SHADY

Shade-Loving

Perennials for

Season-Long

Color

BORDER

C. Colston Burrell Editor

FOR THE
ADVANCE
MENT OF
BOTANY
AND THE
SERVICE OF
THE CITY

BROOKLYN
BOTANIC
GARDEN
PUBLICATIONS
· MCMXCVIII ·

Janet Marinelli
SERIES EDITOR

Beth Hanson
MANAGING EDITOR

Bekka Lindstrom
ART DIRECTOR

Stephen K-M. Tim
VICE PRESIDENT, SCIENCE, LIBRARY & PUBLICATIONS

Judith D. Zuk
PRESIDENT

Elizabeth Scholtz
DIRECTOR EMERITUS

Handbook #155

Copyright © 1998, 2002 by Brooklyn Botanic Garden, Inc.

Handbooks in the *21st-Century Gardening Series,* formerly *Plants & Gardens,*
are published quarterly at 1000 Washington Ave., Brooklyn, NY 11225.

Subscription included in Brooklyn Botanic Garden subscriber membership dues ($35.00 per year).

ISBN # 1-889538-55-8

Printed in China

Table of Contents

The Shady Border

BY C. COLSTON BURRELL

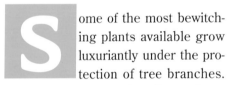

Some of the most bewitching plants available grow luxuriantly under the protection of tree branches. Wood anemones, epimediums, bugbanes, and toad lilies create intricate tapestries under flowering shrubs and trees. Herbaceous perennials form the ground layer of a woodland, sheltered by shrubs, taller understory trees, and a towering canopy. In each vegetation layer, you can grow beautiful species to enhance your shady border. These discrete layers, so vividly arrayed in a natural woodland, can be planted together in vertical as well as horizontal patterns, allowing gardeners plenty of latitude when combining plants.

In the shady border, as in the sunny border, it is the effect created by interesting or unusual combinations of flowers, foliage, and fruits that creates lasting impressions. A bank of forest-green moss beautifully displays the silvery spears of a clump of wild ginger. A colorful carpet of trout lilies, phlox, bluebells, and

Under the protection of tree branches, some of the most bewitching plants available grow luxuriantly, producing stunning color and textural combinations and memorable garden pictures.

bleeding-hearts announce the arrival of spring. The huge leaves of aralia cast elaborate shadows over a carpet of wild ginger. In the glow just after sunset, a bank of lime-green fronds of hayscented fern seems illuminated from within.

In spring, flowering in the shady border reaches its zenith. From late March through May scores of shade-loving plants bloom in the spring sunshine. Early snowdrops dangle in the first warm breezes, which encourage the flowers of hellebores, trilliums, bluebells, and primroses. The pristine white flowers shed from the horizontal branches of a silverbell rain down on artful combinations of wild azaleas, foamflowers, merrybells, shooting stars, dwarf iris, and unfurling green fronds. You can achieve stunning color combinations when you choose your shade plants carefully; seek out cultivars of favorite wildflowers to provide just the right effect. Creeping phlox *(Phlox stolonifera)*, for example, is available in pale or shocking pink, blue, purple, or white. Given the range of color choices, you can choose the cultivar that maximizes the visual impact of the plant combination you are creating.

More than anything, it is summer's foliage that draws me to shaded places. Though flowers take their turn, it is the thousand shades of green that delight the eye for most of the season. Chartreuse, celadon, emerald, and beryl only begin to describe the variety of shades that an uninitiated eye calls "green." The delicate fronds of ferns, the fine-textured fountains of sedges and grasses, the tropical luxuriance of aralias, and the bold texture of umbrella leaf create a tapestry of combinations rich enough to rival any sunny border or bedding scheme. Leaf shapes range from strap-shaped to arrowhead-shaped to rounded to dissected; leaf textures vary from bold to fine.

In late summer and autumn, the blooms of goldenrods, toad lilies, and bugbanes accent the brilliant colors of autumn foliage. The decorative fruits of perennials and shrubs—baneberry, blue cohosh, jack-in-the-pulpit, Solomon's plume, viburnums, beautyberry—add spots of color. Drying seedheads and showy pods also add interest.

In this handbook you will find ideas on creating a shady border in a variety of situations, from the edge of a mature woodland to a single shade tree, even the shadow cast by a building. Gardening is a partnership with nature, a participation in natural processes. To garden effectively, you must first understand the ground rules. In "Manipulating Light Levels" and "The Challenge of Shaded Soils," you'll learn how to work with low light exposures, root competition, and other typical conditions. The shady border peaks in spring, but it is possible to extend the season with flowers, foliage, and decorative fruits. "Designing the Shady Border" explains how to create striking plant combinations in every season.

Finally, in the "Encyclopedia of Shade Perennials," you'll find extensive information about 70 dramatic shade plants for every kind of shady border—dry shade, moist shade, and wet shade. Each entry includes suggestions on how to combine plants to maximize the impact of foliage and bloom. And because the shady border can—unlike its sunny counterpart—include complex combinations of woody as well as herbaceous plants, a list of 60 additional shrubs, flowering trees, and shade trees provides suggestions for spectacular companion plantings.

MANIPULATING

Light Levels

IF YOU HAVE the opportunity to garden beneath the shelter and

BY JUDY SPRINGER

shade of mature trees, you are lucky indeed. The very trees that produce shade will also provide privacy, structure, and year-round interest. They moderate temperature and light, creating a protected site, a restful sanctuary where you can watch changing light patterns alter the appearance of the landscape. In a shady border, there is less weeding than in sun, and gardening in comfort is possible, even on a hot summer day. Finally, shade gardeners get the chance to grow a wonderful selection of plants that require less than full sun.

While a bit of cover from the sun can definitely be an advantage, gardening in a dense wood is also a challenge. It's not hard to figure out why very little grows in deep shade. A high, impenetrable canopy can block out so much light that ground-level plants cannot photosynthesize successfully—so they can't survive, much less thrive. Mature trees are so good at absorbing available water and nutrients that little is left over for smaller plants.

Fortunately, not all shade is the kind that starves out smaller plants: Shade can range from light to deep; it can be dark and unbroken, or dappled; it can be cast by plants or man-made structures. Some types of shade provide much better growing conditions than others; the best kinds of shade for growing the widest range of plants fall in the middle ranges, and are often described as light to medium, partial, or dappled shade.

Plants grow well and look the best in "light shade"—about half a day of sun and half a day of shade. If you have morning sun and afternoon shade, most plants described in catalogs as "good for shade" will grow beautifully for you. It is in these brighter shady situations that "shade-tolerant" plants produce a good flush of foliage and the best flowering display. (If you have morning shade and intense afternoon sun, the same plants may look stressed or burned, particularly in the South.) But nature is always working against gardeners with light shade. Trees and shrubs are constantly gaining stature and girth, blotting out the sun and threatening to reduce light to unsatisfactory levels.

Cutting your way to bright shade

The key to a great border under a canopy of trees lies in the judicious use of chainsaw, pole pruner, hand saw, loppers, and hand pruners. Use these to let enough sunlight into your garden so that the plants grow well yet the unique benefits of shade remain. Many plants that will merely survive in medium to heavy shade will thrive if light levels are increased.

To brighten up your garden, start by removing damaged, unhealthy, or ugly trees, or those that have dense surface roots such as those of beech, birch, and red maple. Next, remove saplings that don't have enough space to grow, and then remove or limb up enough of the remaining trees to achieve varying degrees of light to medium shade throughout your garden. Then go back again and thin out any understory trees, brush, or shrubs that block light without making a real contribution to the attractiveness of the site.

Turning a sunny, barren spot into a shady border requires more patience. When developing this kind of site, use a variety of trees, evergreen and deciduous, that will eventually provide the desired shade, and serve as good "bones" for a new garden. Select trees and shrubs that don't produce heavy surface roots such as oaks, hickory, and other nut trees. Avoid most maples. Small trees such as Japanese maples, dogwoods, redbuds, and pawpaw are easy

---

SHADES OF SHADE

Deciding what constitutes the different degrees of shade is a fairly subjective endeavor—and one that's always open to discussion. Here are the terms commonly used to describe shades of shade.

■ An area that gets bright to full sun for all but a few hours of the day is said to be in *light shade.*

■ Areas with bright light or sunshine for roughly half of the day and shade for the other half are in *partial shade.*

■ When the sun is obstructed for most of the day there is *full shade.*

■ Near-total shade, which is too dark for healthy plant growth except for the most shade-tolerant species, is *dense shade.*

Use your chainsaw, pole pruner, hand saw, loppers, and hand pruners to let enough sunlight into your garden so that your plants can thrive.

Urban gardeners may not be able to change existing light levels, but can choose plants that are best suited to their light conditions.

to work under because their roots are deep. Look for plants that display unusual spring or fall color, that flower or fruit unusually early or late, or that have evergreen foliage, interesting bark, or good silhouettes, and shape them to suit the space as they mature.

Stagger the heights of individual plants in the canopy. If you have closely planted trees of equal height, almost no light will penetrate, but if you use plants of varying heights, sunlight can penetrate clear to the woodland floor and provide the dappled, changing patterns that are most desirable in a shady setting.

The right plants for each low-light site

Shade gardening can be tricky in that it is sometimes difficult to tell just how much sunlight a particular spot in a shady area gets. Don't be afraid to move plants that aren't growing well. Watch plants closely, and if they look stressed by too much light, move them to deeper shade. If they look weak or spindly, move them to a brighter spot, or to the edge of the shady area. If you can't find the right spot for a plant, compost it and try something else.

Shade gardeners must provide the moisture and fertilizer a heavy planting of trees and shrubs demands, and then even more for the garden underneath. Since tree and shrub root systems are much more extensive than those of annuals and perennials, they will absorb what they need, leaving their less aggressive plant partners to get by as best they can. To ensure sufficient moisture for all your plants, make sure that watering remains easy as your garden matures. Install hose bibs, sprinklers, overhead watering, semi-permanent hoses, or leaky pipes wherever possible; whatever money you put toward easy watering will be money well spent.

Shade gardens in the city

If you are an urban gardener working with shade produced by nearby buildings, you cannot change existing light levels, but by carefully analyzing your exposure and hours of light and shade, you can choose plants that are best suited to your conditions. In some cases, reflected light from nearby buildings can be highly beneficial: It may produce higher light levels than you anticipate, and help plants grow more evenly because they don't have to stretch for light. As in other shade gardens, be sure to have a variety of pruning tools on hand, because plants growing in lower light need constant pruning and shaping to keep them from getting leggy and sparse as they reach for any available light.

Whatever you do, don't give up on your shady areas just because they require slightly different strategies from those you are most familiar with. The rewards of shade gardening will grow on you, I promise.

THE CHALLENGE OF
Shaded Soils

S HADE GARDENING
is both an opportunity
and a challenge. Gar-
deners have the opportunity to create an overall effect of serenity and
peace by emphasizing the beauty of
leaf color, form, and texture—often
in the absence of showy, colorful
flowers. The challenge is to achieve

BY CHARLES & MARTHA OLIVER

this effect while working with the poor soils and other difficult conditions that
can predominate in shady sites. What follows are some suggestions for working
with the conditions you've inherited, and to help your plants grow as well as they
can in those conditions.

Most shade comes from trees, and trees have enormous root systems. When
visualizing the root system of any tree, imagine a root mass at least the equal of the
above-ground trunk and branches; some trees, especially those in dry areas, have
root systems that are much larger than the canopy. These extensive root systems
are fierce competitors for soil moisture and nutrients, and the shallow and limited
root systems of small perennials can't hope to compete successfully.

Cycles of moisture and dryness

Many herbaceous perennials have an elegant way of skirting the competition.
When conditions become dry and shady, and air temperatures exceed 85° F.,
ephemeral plants can't draw moisture out of the ground fast enough to prevent wilt-
ing; maintaining a herbaceous top is too risky, so they slough off their stems and
leaves. The plants do not die, but become temporarily dormant—which is why

Shade gardeners can create an overall effect of serenity—and can do so while working with poor soils and other difficult conditions in shady sites.

Enhance your soil's water-holding capacity by mulching with leaf mold, compost, or well-rotted manure.

they're called ephemeral. Virginia bluebell *(Mertensia virginica)*, for example, always discards its leaves by June, drawing moisture into the thick roots, which act as a reservoir for the plant.

A woodland garden's cycles of moisture and drought are very predictable, and plants that thrive there have adapted to these conditions. In spring, abundant rainfall is the signal for spring ephemerals to come up and bloom; often this coincides with the greatest light levels, as the leaves of deciduous trees are just emerging. The woodland plants rush to bloom and seed; many of the loveliest natives are in this early group. By the time the leafy canopy is spread over their heads, their season's work is done and they are giving way to other plants more able to cope with drier, shadier conditions. Not all woodland plants are ephemerals, however. Many plants, including certain asters, white snakeroot, and goldenrod, persist through the season and wait until autumn to bloom.

In summer, soils can get quite dry. Evapo-transpiration from tree leaves can pull hundreds of gallons of water from the ground every day. The most successful dry shade plants—ferns, mosses, *Symphytum grandiflorum,* epimediums, and hostas—have evolved large fleshy roots, leathery leaves, and other strategies to help them compete with thirsty trees and to cut down on moisture loss.

Amending the soil

The surest way for gardeners to provide shade plants with an adequate supply of moisture is to amend the soil, as organic matter helps soils hold moisture. A good woodland soil should contain large quantities of organic matter in the form of humus (rotted leaves and twigs). In a soil heavy with clay or sand and with little organic matter, plants may find it difficult to thrive.

Enhance your soil's water-holding capacity by spreading several inches of leaf mold, compost, and well-rotted manure or wood chips over the surface of the soil and turning it in to the depth of a spading fork. If roots are thick, tangled, and fibrous, it may be impossible to dig in; if so, pile on the mulch and plant in that. For soil that has been "strip-mined" and then run over by heavy machinery, add liberal amounts of rotted wood chips and leaf mold; this type of soil needs lots of amending, so keep a heavy mulch of wood chips, shredded bark, or shredded leaves on the garden and renew it as it rots into humus at soil level.

Never use freshly ground wood chips or sawdust. As these materials rot they will deplete the soil of nitrogen; plants will yellow (the first danger signal) then die. If possible, buy loads of chips and allow them to sit for a year before use.

SHADY BORDERS FOR THE PACIFIC NORTHWEST

Gardeners in the Pacific Northwest need not go far from home to experience nature's best shade gardens: A day's hike in the Cascades will teach the observant gardener much about design and planting. Firs and cedars tower overhead, shading alders, vine maples, and other native trees, while below, Oregon grape and huckleberry, maidenhair and sword ferns inhabit the forest floor. Wildflowers including trilliums, bunchberry, vanilla leaf, and goatsbeard light up this natural woodland garden.

Although gardeners here complain about the wet winters and often-dry summers, our generous rainfall assures lush growth and abundant, verdant shade gardens. While plants in natural settings have adapted to this unique climate, gardeners often fail to recognize that a newly planted shade garden will need regular watering until plants are well rooted and a leafy canopy develops; established gardens may also need watering in the dry months.

Soil conditions are extremely variable: Volcanic mountain ranges, alluvial deposits, and glacial movement sculpted the Northwest, leaving a rich mix of soils from silt to heavy clay over hard pan. Soils on the west side of the Cascade Range and on the coast are acidic. In general, pest and disease problems are few—but slugs seem to thrive in our heavy clay soil and on the lush vegetation that it supports, and are a constant challenge, especially in the shade garden.

—Lucy Hardiman

Most woodland shade plants prefer neutral or slightly acid soil—among them trillium.

Soil pH

Your soil's pH—its acidity or alkalinity—may limit the types of plants you can grow, and it's far easier to choose plants suited to your soil type than to try to change it. (In soil buffered by a lot of organic matter, pH is less critical.) Rhododendrons and azaleas will grow in very acid soil, as will a whole range of other plants including clethra, tiarella, and shield and cinnamon ferns. But in neutral or slightly acid soil many more kinds of plants will grow; in fact, most woodland shade plants prefer this type of soil—among them trillium, great merrybells, baneberry, wild ginger, and wood and Christmas ferns. And then there are plants that prefer a neutral to limy soil (maidenhair ferns, primroses, and wood poppies, shooting stars, and twinleaf, for example), which are found in nature on limestone ledges. If you want to grow these plants and the soil is acidic, sprinkle ground limestone around them as you plant.

Shallow roots and other impediments

Some trees are better to garden under than others. Norway and silver maples, apples, and beech trees all have very shallow, almost surface, roots. Lawn grasses will not grow under these trees, so choose drought-tolerant groundcovers or other plants that will adapt well. Try *Symphytum grandiflorum,* a comfrey relative that produces hanging, pale yellow bells in April, and dark green leaves all season. Epimediums are also good choices for dry shade. Ferns for dry shade include marginal wood fern, male fern, and New York fern.

Some other good choices to grow under trees with shallow roots are *Cyclamen coum* or *Cyclamen hederifolium;* these need moisture in winter and early spring, but very dry conditions in summer. Plant cyclamen corms within the root zone of a beech tree, where conditions will be just right for these charming woodlanders, as beech roots slurp up any moisture from summer rains. Plant nursery-grown corms three inches deep, cutting a hole in the fibrous tree roots with a knife (if necessary) and cover the corm with a light mulch. The flowers and leaves will pierce the mulch from below with no trouble.

In the worst case—very acid soil under tangled maple roots—elevate the garden in raised beds or planters; keep the beds at least 6 feet from the base of the trunk so that you don't damage the tree. Frames of fieldstone, railroad ties, cement block, or brick can be filled with prepared soil mixes for woodland plants: Compost mixed with coarse sand and topsoil in equal proportions will cre-

SHADY BORDERS FOR THE NORTHEAST AND MID-ATLANTIC

In the mid-Atlantic region (Delaware, the District of Columbia, and Maryland), moderate temperatures last from mid-April to mid-October, so gardeners can grow a wide range of plants. Search your garden for microclimates hospitable to more demanding candidates; in a protected niche you may be able to grow marginally tender plants like calanthes and camellias while many of the minor bulbs—Japanese arisaemas, hardy cyclamen, and woodland iris—like a corner with good drainage. Repeated spring freezes and thaws can heave plants with weak root systems, so plant and transplant in early fall. Water during inevitable periods of summer drought; your plants will cope better with heat and look better, too. Soils in the mid-Atlantic region are generally fertile, but often low in organic matter.

The farther north you go, the shorter the growing season and the colder the winter. Massachusetts, New Hampshire, Vermont, and Maine gardeners should pay close attention to hardiness ratings so as not to waste money on plants that can't possibly survive. Cooler summer temperatures may mean that less watering is required, while winter's snow cover provides valuable protection. In both the Northeast and the mid-Atlantic areas, high heat and summer humidity can cause mildew and other fungal problems, and various forms of crown and root rot; work to improve air circulation and provide good drainage. Northeastern soils are often thin and acidic. Rather than undertaking massive soil amendment, grow plants that are adapted to these soils. Your success rate will be much higher.

—Judy Springer

ate conditions so prime that the plants will be lush and enormous. Of course the tree roots will sense the bounty and find their way into the planters, too, unless you put a barrier across the bottom. Landscape fabric won't stop most tree roots; you may need a solid floor; several layers of 6-mil plastic sheeting should do the trick.

If you have just one large tree in your garden, you may still have a soil problem: Trees grown in the lawn or out in the open often have wide, shallow root systems. Only the shade cast by a building will not be accompanied by a root problem—but these gardens may have their own set of troubles: dense shade, or too much water if the slope or the edges of the building channel water there. To increase drainage, add coarse sand, fine gravel, or grit to the soil; if the soil is very moist, you will be limited to plants that tolerate soggy conditions.

When to plant

Once the soil is amended, it's time to think about planting. Bulbs are easy to plant: Dig a hole four times the depth of the bulb and place the rooted end of the dormant bulb firmly into the base of the hole. Cover with soil. Wait until spring, when the new growth emerges, to fertilize.

Plant perennials before or after active growth; plant primroses, for example, in early spring or after blooming, when they die back. Dig a hole large enough so that you can spread the roots out. If you are planting potted material, make sure the hole is deep enough so that you can place the plant slightly deeper than it was growing in the pot. If the soil is dry, fill the hole with water before planting, and wait for the water to drain away. Then water to settle the soil after planting. Mulch with well-rotted wood chips or leaf mold around, but not up, the plant's stem.

Never plant in soggy soil, because you can compact it and destroy tilth and structure while working it. Plant when the soil is drier than usual, during periods when rain isn't frequent, or temporarily cover the planting area with plastic to repel rain or roof water to keep the soil workable.

Maintaining your plants

If you've chosen plants well-suited to the site—paying special attention to pH and moisture levels—you'll have fewer maintenance chores than you would in a sunny herbaceous border. You won't be dividing plants in spring and summer, because most woodland plants don't require the constant division that perennials for the sunny border do. Foamflowers and creeping phlox simply move to another site if they need additional space, using their own method of travel (stolons on top of the ground). These perennials will form large clumps or drifts of plants; should you wish to increase your holdings more swiftly, lift small clumps after flowering and move them to a new site.

You shouldn't have to water your shade garden often unless you've sited plants in the wrong spot. During periods of drought, though, watering can make a good deal of difference in your garden. Watering with a sprinkler is not ideal, as it will encourage plants to send feeder roots to the top inch of soil, making them more vulnerable to heat and dry conditions. Water thoroughly and deeply, soaking the ground with more water than you think the plants need. An underground soaker hose on a timer is ideal, and you will lose less water to evaporation than you would with a sprinkler system. Water at night to give plants and soil more time to draw up the moisture.

Weed your garden to keep out unwanted plants that try to seed in. Vigilance with weeds is the best strategy; pull them before they seed next year's crop. Dis-

SHADY BORDERS FOR THE SOUTHEAST

Most of the Southeast is blessed with a long growing season, a warm climate, and abundant rainfall, although rainfall patterns vary: Winter and spring are generally wetter than summer or fall. Humidity is high during the growing season, reducing the evaporation of water from leaves and soil and mitigating the stressful effects of dry shade.

Southeastern soils tend toward acidity, and vary from nutrient-rich red clay hill soils to anaerobic blue, yellow, or white clays, to infertile coastal sands, to shallow, stony mountain soils, to rich, black, well-drained Mississippi delta loess.

Warm night temperatures characteristic of the Southeast pose unique problems for shade gardeners. Increased nighttime respiration limits growth in many garden species and hot nights encourage diseases such as Southern blight *(Sclerotium rolfsii)*.

Gardening in shade is the natural lot of the Southeastern gardener, because we garden on land that, if left untended, would revert to forest. In fact, local forests are excellent models for shade gardens, with a wealth of well-adapted native species, both ephemeral and persistent. Southeastern gardens also welcome many plants native to warm temperate and subtropical Asia.

—Edith Eddleman

The shade garden, modeled on an established forest system, requires less maintenance than the sunny herbaceous border, the rock garden, or the vegetable garden.

SHADY BORDERS FOR THE MIDWEST

The region known as the Midwest stretches from the edge of the eastern deciduous forest west to the rain shadow of the Rocky Mountains, and from boreal Canada south to Oklahoma. Within this vast region, diversity—in vegetation, soils, and climate—is the rule.

Deciduous woodlands are dominated by oak (bur, white, and red), hickory, basswood, sugar maple, and ash, and the forest floor below is carpeted with wildflowers. The mineral soils are rich clay or silt loams, topped by a thin mantle of organic soil; many are influenced by limestone bedrock and thus are slightly acidic to slightly alkaline. Gardeners in this region have an embarrassment of riches, and except where subsurface clay is the only soil, gardening is easy. Massive amounts of organic matter and a strong back will eventually transform clay into soil for shade plants. Pine, oak, and hickory cover the poorer soils, where nutrients and water can be scarce, but with the addition of organic matter, drought-tolerant shade plants will thrive. In the coniferous forests, perennials with persistent leaves such as partridgeberry and cold-adapted plants such as beadlily combine to make glorious gardens.

Winter temperatures can drop to -30°F. for weeks on end, and summer temperatures may soar to the mid-90°s F. When moist Gulf air is pulled in, the atmosphere drips with humidity. Winters in the northern reaches of the region generally have the consistent snow cover that makes gardening with herbaceous plants easier than it is for more southern neighbors in zone 5. The vagaries of climate severely limit the woody vegetation in zones 3 and 4.

—*C. Colston Burrell*

covering the source of weed seeds can be helpful. A large weedy field close to your woodland garden, for instance, will be a continual source of airborne seeds and aggravate your maintenance problem. Birds will also carry seeds into your garden in their guts; most of these will be tree seeds, so hand-pulling can usually keep the problem in check.

The shady border, overall, requires less maintenance than the sunny herbaceous border, the rock garden, or the vegetable garden, because it is modeled on a climax vegetation—a stable evolutionary system. The herbaceous plants of established forests change little over time, and a garden modeled on a forest will provide less trouble and more rewards than any other type of garden.

CHAPTER THREE

DESIGNING THE

Shady Border

IF GARDENERS are such an intrepid lot, willing to move mountains of soil, lay miles of brick and stone, and shovel tons of manure, why does the mere mention of shade cause so many to quake in their boots? Gardeners from novice to knowledgeable assume that a shady border can never be as colorful and visually interesting as a sunny one. They also fear that small trees, shrubs, and perennials won't perform as well in shady situations as they do in the sun. But, contrary to popular belief, well-designed shade gardens are as lush and colorful as their brethren in full sun.

BY LUCY L. HARDIMAN

Shade gardens have a different feel and sensibility from gardens in full sun. The canopy shades, cools, and protects perennials and smaller shrubs in the understory. Light in the shade garden is dappled and less direct, so colors seem more intense. Plants are less likely to be stressed or burned by the sun. Green takes on new importance as its many hues intermingle, providing visual continuity. Leaf and flower forms and textures are more obvious against a field of green. But, most of all, shade gardens are serene and peaceful, quiet retreats for the visitor and gardener alike.

Color in a new light

Whether in a shady or sunny border, color has the power to evoke any number of emotions. Contrasting colors, such as yellow and violet, are stimulating and dramatic when used together. Harmonious colors—those adjacent to each other on the color wheel, like red and orange, blend, creating soothing, softer pictures.

Shade gardens have a distinct feel and sensibility: Light is dappled, and leaf and flower forms and textures are more obvious against the intermingled hues of green.

In a shady border, indirect sunlight makes colors appear saturated; in bright sunlight, the same colors can lose their clarity and intensity and become washed out.

Colors derived from red and orange are considered hot, while those based on blue are considered cool. Bear in mind that colors look different in the shade than they do in the sun: Bright sunlight diminishes the strength of color, causing pastels to bleach out and lose their intensity and subduing the clarity of red, blue, and yellow. In a shade garden, light is diffuse and colors retain their saturation.

Green is a color too, and nowhere is this more apparent—and important—than in the shade garden. Integrate every shade of green imaginable in your shade-garden design. Bright chartreuse greens illuminate shady places. Medium greens—nature's own background colors—are neutral and ease the transition between contrasting colors. Blue-greens create the illusion of depth and can make small spaces appear larger. Dark, inky black or olive greens provide a contrasting backdrop for lighter, brighter foliage and blooms. Placing a blue-green hosta behind the bright green foliage and chartreuse yellow bloom of lady's mantle will create tension and color contrast, while planting a pink astilbe in front of the same hosta will produce a different look and feeling.

Use foliage to create an illusion of brightness. Light-colored leaves or those with cream or white margins or variegation reflect light, making the surrounding area appear brighter. The yellow- and green-striped foliage of Japanese ribbon grass

Blue-green foliage (above) creates the illusion of depth in the garden while bright chartreuse greens (right) command attention.

paired with the electrifying foliage of the golden barberry and the silver-gray and cream foliage of a variegated hosta has enough wattage to light up an entire garden.

When you find a few color combinations that you like, repeat them throughout the garden to unify the space and create a sense of movement and flow.

Valuing leaf texture & form

Keep not only foliage color, but plant form and texture in mind when selecting plant associations. Juxtaposing different leaf textures and forms adds a critical component to the shade-garden tapestry. Many shade plants have leaves with large surface areas, an adaptation that allows for maximum photosynthesis in lower light conditions. Another benefit of larger foliage is the opportunity to create dramatic visual effects in the shade garden. Small, delicate foliage will provide a contrast when planted next to larger leaf forms. A maidenhair fern with its elegant, finely dissected fronds, for example, makes more of an impact if planted in front of a dwarf conifer than in front of another fern or plant with similar foliage.

Contrasting forms can also be used effectively in the shade garden. For example, planting a late-blooming monkshood, with very sharply incised leaves and a tall, spiky flower stalk, with a hydrangea, substantial and dense with weighty flower heads, adds dimension and visual interest as well

Many shade plants, like hostas, have leaves with large surface areas allowing not only for maximum photosynthesis but dramatic visual effects.

as extending the bloom season. Plants with large, deep-green leaves, such as rhododendrons, will read as dark and bulky, while a variegated *Kerria*, with its pom-pom flowers, open habit, and serrated leaf will seem light, open, and airy.

Complex combinations

Shade gardens are complex combinations of very diverse planting materials ranging from tiny groundcovers that form a living carpet on the garden floor to the towering trees that form the canopy or upper story of the garden. Bulbs, perennials, and evergreen and deciduous shrubs are the workhorses of the mid-layer of the garden. When you can thoughtfully and artfully weave all these elements together, the shade garden conveys a sense of lushness and abundance, a oneness with nature.

TREES From a design perspective, trees are the major "bones" of the garden,

Plants with contrasting hues, forms, and textures—like the *Athyrium, Aquilegia*, and *Rodgersia* above—can add dimension and visual interest to your shady border.

defining and framing spaces and serving as focal points. Columnar shapes draw the eye upward, while trees with rounded canopies appear horizontal, and weeping and prostrate forms lead the eye to the understory and ground plane.

Trees provide relief and protection from the sun and cast shade on the plants below. Canopy trees also provide enclosure, creating intimacy and a ceiling for outdoor rooms. Use deciduous trees that leaf out late in the spring to give understory and ground-plane plants a period of full light in which early spring-blooming bulbs and perennials can prosper.

Depending on the size and density of their foliage, different trees will cast different types and densities of shade. Intermittent sunlight can pierce the canopy of trees with small leaves and open, layered habits, reaching the understory plants below. Japanese maple, mountain ash, katsura, Japanese snowbell, oak, Himalayan birch, small-flowered magnolia, Persian parrotia, and Asian dogwoods are choice trees for the shade garden, with their shapely forms and an exciting array of seasonal bark, berry, flower, and foliage displays. Among indigenous North American trees well suited for the shade garden are redbud, with colorful bloom and clear yellow fall color; serviceberry, with white flowers and red-orange fall foliage; and Washington hawthorn, which has a tidy, layered habit and bunches of clear orange berries in the fall. Trees that cast dense shade, deplete the soil of nutrients and water, and become too large are poor choices for the garden. Among these are Indian bean trees, chestnuts, big-leaf maples, and full-sized evergreen magnolias.

Conifers are the anchors of the winter garden, their elegant evergreen shapes contrasting with the stark outlines of the bare but beautiful forms of deciduous trees and shrubs, so be sure to include them in your shady border. Conifers cast dense, year-round shade and should be sited accordingly on the periphery of the garden or on the north side of the site. Smaller, upright coniferous forms such as incense cedar and Nootka cypress take up less space and cast less shade, creating better growth conditions for plants in the understory and ground plane. Although many of these needled evergreens are too large for residential gardens, the many smaller or dwarf forms can work well.

SHRUBS Shrubs, large and small, deciduous and evergreen, create a backdrop for the more ephemeral perennials and serve as a foil for groundcovers. Use them like walls to divide spaces, provide privacy, and screen unattractive views. When choosing shrubs, think about their year-round attributes: Do they bloom, have good fall color, produce berries, have exfoliating bark, or appealing fragrance? If a shrub meets two or more of these criteria, consider including it in the garden.

The best known of the shade-tolerant shrubs are rhododendrons and azaleas,

Many herbaceous perennials have unusual and eye-catching foliage, including *Ligularia* and the versatile hostas; they are the stars of the shade garden.

workhorses that contribute both colorful blooms and interesting foliage. Camellias, both the winter- and spring-blooming species, offer colorful flowers and shiny foliage where winters are mild. Sweet box blooms in January, its insignificant, tiny blossoms releasing an incredibly sweet fragrance; it also has evergreen, glossy foliage and black berries, making it a quintessential year-round plant. Many hollies have evergreen foliage, small blooms, and produce prodigious amounts of fruit. Witchhazels, fulfilling the role of either large shrub or small multi-stemmed tree, magically cover their stems with fragrant blooms in winter and also put on a colorful show in the fall. Winter hazels, witchhazel relatives, light up the shade garden in early spring with fragrant, buttery yellow flowers that are perfect companions for early bulbs or perennials with blue blooms. Drooping leucothoe's spreading, graceful habit contrasts with some of the more spiky, upright shrub forms. The species is a blaze of red in the autumn while another form has lively green and cream foliage.

No shade border could be complete without a hydrangea. These archetypal plants are trendy now, and there's a form to fit any size or style garden—from two-foot dwarf to ten-foot giant, from mophead to lacecap. Sweet pepperbush, a woodland native, is wind- and salt-tolerant, making it a perfect choice for coastal as well as inland gardens. It produces sweetly scented white or pink spires in the late summer that attract more than 100 different insects. Try combining sweet pepperbush, which blooms in August, with pink or white Japanese anemones and a white hydrangea to add a touch of elegance to the late summer garden.

PERENNIALS Just as they are in the sunny border, herbaceous perennials are the ephemeral stars of the shade garden, many with unusual and eye-catching foliage. Ornamental rhubarb and rodgersia, with their large leaves and wands of bloom, add drama and an architectural element to the garden. No plant is more emblematic of shade gardening than the hosta. Modern hybridizing has produced hundreds of varieties with fabulous pleated foliage in a rainbow of colors from gray to chartreuse with every possible variegation of green, gold, cream, and white. False spiraea or astilbe, with its incised foliage and soft plumes, creates contrast and tension when paired with hosta. Meadow rue, columbine, and bleeding-heart have soft, ferny textures and therefore should be placed near the verge of the woodland or border where they can be appreciated up close. Christmas roses—hellebores—begin blooming in February, brightening the winter landscape with pendant bells of white, pink, and purple. No shade garden would be complete without ferns. Native ferns are found in a range of habitats from moist woodlands to dry and shady sites.

The spring wildflower display in North American woodland gardens is glorious. Japanese primroses and Virginia bluebells are entrancing; the heart-shaped blooms of the bleeding-heart enchanting. Elegant shooting stars, dog-tooth violets, and trilliums nose through the duff on the forest floor. Peering under the shiny, heart-shaped foliage of wild ginger for blooms is, for some, a rite of spring.

Year-round interest

Careful planning and plant selection in the design phase to insure year-round color and interest is as important in the shady garden as it is in the sunny border. Spring is the season of rejuvenation and rebirth as the early bulbs and spring-blooming perennials poke through the dark earth and burst into bloom, followed by the unfurling of fresh new foliage on the shrubs and trees. Summer signifies abundance, with a plethora of perennials and shrubs in full bloom anchored by lush foliage forms. The shorter days and longer nights of autumn usher in the kaleidoscope colors of fall as the foliage turns and berries ripen. Winter bares the soul of the garden, exposing its bones for all to see. With the advent of the new year, the witchhazels and hellebores sneak into bloom and the shade garden comes alive with the promise of what is to come.

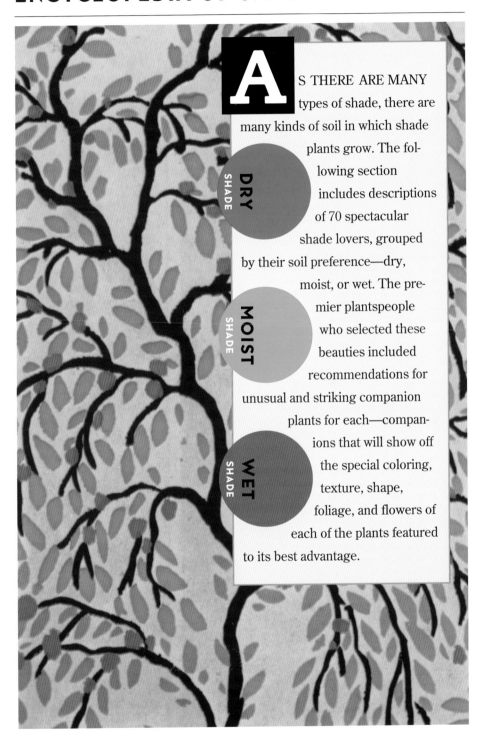

AS THERE ARE MANY types of shade, there are many kinds of soil in which shade plants grow. The following section includes descriptions of 70 spectacular shade lovers, grouped by their soil preference—dry, moist, or wet. The premier plantspeople who selected these beauties included recommendations for unusual and striking companion plants for each—companions that will show off the special coloring, texture, shape, foliage, and flowers of each of the plants featured to its best advantage.

DRY SHADE

MOIST SHADE

WET SHADE

Perennials for Dry Shade

BY EDITH EDDLEMAN

This section includes just a fraction of the plants that will not just survive but thrive in dry shade. They are some of the toughest plants found in nature, and also among the most beautiful. These plants have lots to offer in the way of texture, leaf shape, flower color, and habit. They may be combined in soothing, harmonious garden pictures or in exciting juxtapositions of leaf, shape, and color—the choice is yours to enjoy. Your success with these rugged beauties will be ensured by thorough soil preparation, yearly topdressing with compost and manure, fertilization if needed, annual mulching, and regular watering during periods of prolonged drought.

FERNS, GRASSES, AND SEDGES

Carex morrowii 'Variegata'
VARIEGATED JAPANESE SEDGE
NATIVE HABITAT AND RANGE: Woods in low mountains in Japan
USDA HARDINESS ZONE: 5 to 9
OUTSTANDING FEATURES: The evergreen leaves are broad for a sedge (½" wide), and dark green edged with creamy white. The plant forms a dense, upright clump. It is a natural exclamation point.
HABIT, USE, AND GOOD COMPANIONS:
Clumps are 12" to 15" tall and can be up to 2' in diameter. This evergreen sedge looks attractive with hostas, evergreen ligularias, and ferns and contrasts well with groundcovers such as silver-leaved

Carex morrowii 'Goldband'

Chasmanthium latifolium

Lamium galeobdolon 'Herman's Pride' or gold-flowered green-and-gold (*Chrysogonum virginianum*).

HOW TO GROW: Tolerates sun or shade in ordinary garden soil. It is seldom necessary to divide clumps, unless more plants are desired. Divide and replant in fall. May grow in zone 4 with protection.

CULTIVARS AND RELATED SPECIES: *Carex morrowii* 'Ice Dance' (zone 5 to 9) looks just like *C. morrowii* 'Variegata' except that its habit is spreading rather than clump-forming. *Carex morrowii* 'Goldband' (zone 5 to 9) is a clump-former whose leaves have much broader white edges. *Carex morrowii* 'Silk Tassel' (zone 5 to 9), also a clump-former, has very narrow, wispy green leaves striped in white, and gives a silvery effect in the garden.

Chasmanthium latifolium
NORTHERN SEA OATS
(Wild Oats, Upland Sea Oats)

NATIVE HABITAT AND RANGE: Low woods, riverbanks, dikes, and ditches in eastern U.S. and northern Mexico

USDA HARDINESS ZONE: 5 to 9

OUTSTANDING FEATURES: The elegant drooping panicles of flattened spikelets, carried on slender leafy culms (stems), are the outstanding feature of this native grass. The inflorescence, which resembles that of its closely related endangered relative *Chasmanthium paniculatum* (coastal sea oats), is particularly beautiful when backlit by the sun.

HABIT, USE, AND GOOD COMPANIONS: This rhizomatous grass can be 2' to 4' tall and flowers in midsummer. Its beautiful texture adds excitement to low-growing plantings of groundcovers such as *Ajuga* or *Vinca*. Plant on banks to add height. It is a vicious seeder, so remove ripe seedheads and dry them for decorative arrangements—or be prepared to weed early the next year. Combines well with large-leaved plants such as hydrangeas, hostas, and bergenias.

HOW TO GROW: Easy to transplant (and difficult to eradicate). In the Southeastern states, its foliage tends to burn in summer in full sun, and plants look sickly, so plant only in shady spots. More tolerant of sun in the northern part of its range.

CULTIVARS AND RELATED SPECIES: No cultivars known. Closely related *C. paniculatum* grows in full sunlight and is limited to coastal dunes. Do not pick the seeds of this endangered species or collect specimens.

Dryopteris erythrosora
AUTUMN FERN

NATIVE HABITAT AND RANGE: Damp mountain woods in Asia

USDA HARDINESS ZONE: 5 to 8

OUTSTANDING FEATURES: Clump-forming evergreen fern with coppery new fronds in spring. The shiny, deep green, leathery fronds are triangular in shape. The sori (clusters of spore cases) on the undersides of the fronds are rusty red.

HABIT, USE, AND GOOD COMPANIONS: The mature clump forms a tufted vase 18" to 2' tall. Use as a foundation planting, or combine with shrubs or in mass plantings with other ferns. Combines well with hostas, *Arum italicum,* wild ginger, and other groundcovers.

HOW TO GROW: Good in shade but can also tolerate some sun. Grows best in well-prepared, humus-enriched woodland soil. Established plants will tolerate dry soil.

CULTIVARS AND RELATED SPECIES: *D. marginalis* (marginal shield fern) is 18" to 24" tall, with dark, evergreen, leathery foliage and a broadly vase-shaped profile. *D. filix-mas* 'Barnesii' grows to 3' tall, with narrow upright fronds, and does well in acid to slightly alkaline soils.

Polystichum polyblepharum
KOREAN TASSEL FERN

NATIVE HABITAT AND RANGE: Rich, acidic woodlands in Japan and southern Korea

USDA HARDINESS ZONE: 5 to 8

OUTSTANDING FEATURES: Its highly attractive deep green, lacy evergreen fronds (slightly lustrous on the top surface) are up to 18" long.

HABIT, USE, AND GOOD COMPANIONS: Finely cut fronds arch gracefully out from a central point, forming a clump 2' wide. Magnificent with tiarella, splendid with hostas, Solomon's seal, woodland iris, and bleeding-hearts. Can be planted as a

Sasa veitchii

specimen or used in large groups. Combines well with small ferns such as southern maidenhair *(Adiantum capillus-veneris)* as well as sedges and shade-tolerant grasses.

HOW TO GROW: Plant in thoroughly prepared, well-drained soil enriched with organic matter. Remove any damaged fronds in spring before new fronds emerge. For mass plantings, space plants 2½' apart on center.

CULTIVARS AND RELATED SPECIES: *Polystichum acrostichoides* (Christmas fern), a native of the U.S., is evergreen with fronds 1' to 2' in length. Individual pinnae (leaflets) resemble Christmas stockings (hence its common name). Tolerates extremely sandy soil, but grows best in humus-rich woodland soils. Despite the fact that it is evergreen, it really benefits from a cutback of old foliage in early spring before the new fronds unfurl.

Sasa veitchii
KUMA BAMBOO GRASS

NATIVE HABITAT AND RANGE: Woods and scrubland in Japan

USDA HARDINESS ZONE: 7 to 9

OUTSTANDING FEATURES: This small bamboo has purple-veined leaves that, in winter, develop broad, papery-white margins, giving the plant a variegated appearance. The leaves are plain green in summer, and are crowded toward the tip of the stems, giving it a graceful, fan-like appearance.

HABIT, USE, AND GOOD COMPANIONS: Culms (stems) are about 2' tall. This is one of the less aggressive rhizomatous bamboo species and can even be an excellent pot plant. In the garden, it makes a striking composition when combined with black bamboo and black mondo grass.

HOW TO GROW: Planted in ordinary to heavy garden soil, it spreads slowly. In fertile or lighter soils, you may wish to contain its roots. Can be cut to the ground (especially if foliage has been damaged by a hard winter), as new culms will emerge in spring.

CULTIVARS AND RELATED SPECIES: *Pleioblastus auricoma (Arundinaria viridistriata)*, running bamboo, is similar but smaller, with wiry stems and terminal fans of narrow, deep green leaves. Plants grow 2'-2½' tall and can be rampant spreaders.

FLOWERING PLANTS

Anemonella thalictroides
RUE ANEMONE

NATIVE HABITAT AND RANGE: Rich woods from northwest Florida to eastern Oklahoma, north to southern New Hampshire and southeast Minnesota

USDA HARDINESS ZONE: 3 to 8

OUTSTANDING FEATURES: Early-flowering spring ephemeral, which usually carries three graceful flowers per stem above dainty lace-like foliage. The flowers, which look like delicate single anemones, are normally white but pink forms are not unusual.

HABIT, USE, AND GOOD COMPANIONS: Upright habit, 6" to 10" in height. Can form clumps. Adequate spring moisture can lengthen the blooming period up to two months. Because rue anemone is ephemeral, it is good to interplant it with evergreen perennials such as *Phlox*

stolonifera and gingers. The pink form looks beautiful with black mondo grass *(Ophiopogon planiscapus* 'Nigrescens').

HOW TO GROW: Tough and long-lived, rue anemone is extremely tolerant of the driest shade and nutrient-poor soil, but is more robust and flowers more profusely in a well-prepared, fertile soil with adequate moisture. After seeds ripen but before the foliage dies down, the sturdy tuberous roots can be easily divided.

CULTIVARS AND RELATED SPECIES: There are many selections of *Anemonella thalictroides*. Those most readily available include 'Schoaff's Double Pink', a double-flowered form with lavender-pink pompom-like flowers (to 6" tall); 'Betty Blake', aka 'Green Dragon', a semi-double form with greenish outer sepals and whitish inner sepals arranged in a whorl like the blades of a pinwheel; and 'Cameo', a form with pale pink, fully double pom-pom flowers.

Arum italicum
ITALIAN ARUM

NATIVE HABITAT AND RANGE: Open woods and scrubland in Southeastern Europe

USDA HARDINESS ZONE: 6 to 10

OUTSTANDING FEATURES: Large, arrowhead-shaped leaves are borne on long petioles (leaf stalks) rising directly from the soil. The most attractive forms have vein patterns outlined in cream. Flowers, which emerge in spring, have large, balloon-like, pale green spathes around a cream-colored spadix. Green berries set in spring and ripen to red-orange in late summer. Foliage is green throughout winter and in summer is dormant; summer dormancy makes it an excellent plant for dry shade.

HABIT, USE, AND GOOD COMPANIONS: Plants grow about 18" tall in nutrient-rich clay soil or soil amended with organic matter, but are much smaller in infertile, sandy soil. Arum tolerates the deep shade of evergreens or buildings, but also grows well in full winter sun. It tolerates both dry and moist shade. Can be grown in combination with stinking hellebore *(Helleborus foetidus)* or snowdrops *(Galanthus* species) in well-drained soils, or around the bases of deciduous shrubs such as yellow-twig dogwood, in wet heavy soils.

HOW TO GROW: The best leaf forms are propagated by division, and should be planted about 1' apart. Arum can also be grown from seeds; collect them as soon as fruits ripen because their fleshy coatings are so attractive to wildlife. Plant seeds about 2" deep directly in the ground after removing the fleshy coating, which retards germination. New plants will emerge the following spring.

CULTIVARS AND RELATED SPECIES: *Arum creticum* has shiny green leaves resembling broad spear tips and a bright yellow spadix rising out of a creamy white calla-like spathe.

Arum italicum 'Pictum'

Asarum arifolium
LITTLE BROWN JUGS

NATIVE HABITAT AND RANGE: Deciduous or pine woods and swamp forests in the southeastern U.S. from Virginia to Florida, Alabama

USDA HARDINESS ZONE: 4 to 9

OUTSTANDING FEATURES: Green arrowhead-shaped leaves (usually spotted and/or veined with silver) persist throughout winter and may turn bronze during that season. The common name refers to the brown, jug-shaped flowers borne in spring at ground level beneath the leaves. *A. arifolium* is one of the larger species of evergreen asarums.

HABIT, USE, AND GOOD COMPANIONS: Grows

DRY SHADE

5" to 8" tall; best used as an accent plant. Handsome combined with Japanese painted fern *(Athyrium niponicum)*, Small's beardstongue *(Penstemon smallii)*, ivy leaf cyclamen *(Cyclamen hederifolium)*, and strawberry geranium *(Saxifraga stolonifera)*.

HOW TO GROW: Plant in humus-enriched, well-prepared soil. Tolerates soils ranging from sand to clay, but will wilt in summer under extreme drought conditions, particularly in sandy soils. Propagate by division in fall.

CULTIVARS AND RELATED SPECIES: *A. virginicum,* (5" to 7") has dark green, heart-shaped evergreen leaves, often with dramatic silver markings. The smaller (3" to 5") *A. minor* also has evergreen, heart-shaped leaves varying in color from pale to medium green; many forms have striking silver patterns on the leaves. *A. shuttleworthii* has small, more rounded green leaves with white veins; 'Calloway' is an outstanding form with silver veins.

Aspidistra elatior
CAST-IRON PLANT

NATIVE HABITAT AND RANGE: Woodlands in China

USDA HARDINESS ZONE: 7 to 10

OUTSTANDING FEATURES: Handsome black-green leaves rise directly from the ground, widening from slender petioles (leaf stalks) to a broad lance shape. Its common name, cast-iron plant, refers to its ability to thrive in tough situations. It tolerates drought, deep dark shade, and even the corners of Victorian drawing-rooms. The flowers, which appear in winter, have eight cream-colored lobes spotted with purple and a claret interior. They are borne at ground level at the base of the plant.

HABIT, USE, AND GOOD COMPANIONS: The tall, elegant leaves of the species can be 2' or more in length. The dramatic ever-green foliage of the cast-iron plant makes it a natural combined with either the finely cut foliage of ferns or the bold leaves of hostas. At the northern end of its range, it is an excellent plant to grow either on the north side of a building or in evergreen shade. Farther south, it can tolerate the greater exposure of deciduous shade.

HOW TO GROW: Divide in spring, but only after the danger of frost is past. In an exceptionally cold winter, cast-iron plant may suffer severe leaf damage, but do not despair. Cut off damaged leaves at ground level, and it will resprout—slowly.

CULTIVARS AND RELATED SPECIES: The leaves of the cultivar 'Variegata' are medium green with uneven white or cream stripes. In 'Asahi' leaves are green, but the center of each leaf tip turns a ghostly white with age. *A. lurida* cultivar 'Milky Way', also known as 'Minor', has shorter leaves and shorter petioles that are more arching than those of the species, giving plants a bushy effect. The green foliage is abundantly speckled with white.

Bletilla striata
CHINESE GROUND ORCHID

NATIVE HABITAT AND RANGE: Dry prairie regions in Japan, China, Tibet

USDA HARDINESS ZONE: 5 to 10

OUTSTANDING FEATURES: An orchid that is easy to grow, and in spring produces racemes of nodding flowers that are carried above the foliage. The flowers, which appear to be dainty miniature forms of the florist's *Cattleya* or corsage orchid, have deep purply pink petals and sepals, and pale pink lips with dark purple markings. Pseudobulbs below ground produce 3 to 5 long, pleated leaves, which remain attractive throughout the growing season.

HABIT, USE, AND GOOD COMPANIONS: Leaves are 8" to 15" long. This orchid actually grows well in partially sunny or shady, dry conditions. Its leaves provide a bold grassy texture, which contrasts pleasingly with hostas or the finely cut foliage of ferns.

HOW TO GROW: Can be propagated from last year's pseudobulbs if these are separated from those of the current year. If cut off and planted in fall, these will resprout the next spring. Space the plants about 1' apart. Plant in soils with good organic content.

CULTIVARS AND RELATED SPECIES: In *B. striata* cultivars 'Variegata' and 'Albo-striata', the outer edge of the leaf blade is white.

Bletilla striata

The cultivar 'Alba' has white flowers. Hybrids of *B. striata* and soft pink *B. formosana* produce plants with flowers of various intermediate shades as well as white-flowered plants. Related species *B. ochracea* has soft yellow flowers and a longer period of bloom, producing flowers from spring through mid-summer.

Chrysogonum virginianum
GREEN-AND-GOLD

NATIVE HABITAT AND RANGE: Open woodlands and forest edges from Pennsylvania south to Florida and Louisiana

USDA HARDINESS ZONE: 5 to 9

OUTSTANDING FEATURES: The cheerful yellow, five-rayed flowers begin to appear in early spring, and can have an extraordinarily long period of bloom. In zones 7 to 9, green-and-gold may bloom for 11 months of the year. Forms low, evergreen clumps with scalloped, slightly hairy, green leaves.

HABIT, USE, AND GOOD COMPANIONS: Stemless or very short-stemmed low (2" to 4") perennial. Can be used as a groundcover. Pretty combined with Small's beardstongue *(Penstemon smallii)*, hostas, or carexes (particularly gold-leaved cultivars). In spring, the rounded yellow flowers form a pleasing contrast to the blue, spiked inflorescences of ajuga (especially the purple-leaved forms). In autumn, its blooms echo the flower color of autumn daffodil *(Sternbergia lutea)*.

HOW TO GROW: Grows best in well-prepared acid to neutral soils (it occurs naturally in well-drained woodland soils). Divide in fall and plant before frost. Will reproduce by seed, but is not an aggressive seeder. Its short height will enable it to escape into lawns. Can grow in fair-

Chrysogonum virginianum

ly heavy deciduous shade or (if well-watered) in full sun. Green-and-gold may be attacked by southern blight *(Sclerotium rolfsii)* when nights are warm. Soil with a high organic content and a cooling layer of mulch helps to protect against this pathogen. Will grow in zone 4 with protection.

CULTIVARS AND RELATED SPECIES: The variety *australe,* which is stoloniferous and hugs the ground, occurs naturally in sandy to rocky woodlands. Cultivar 'Eco Lacquered Spider' (zones 5 to 9) has glossy leaves and runners up to several feet in length. The stolons as well as the leaf bases are purple. It has a short bloom period in spring.

Cyclamen hederifolium
IVY LEAFED CYCLAMEN

NATIVE HABITAT AND RANGE: Open woods and scrubland from the Mediterranean coast of Europe to Iran

USDA HARDINESS ZONE: 5 to 9

OUTSTANDING FEATURES: Small pink flowers with reflexed sepals borne on nodding stems resemble little moths in flight. Plants may begin to flower in mid-summer, but more typically in autumn. Leaves emerge after flowering, remain green throughout winter, and become dormant the next summer. The dark green leaves, usually heavily marbled and/or veined with pale green or silver, may be shaped like ivy,

Cyclamen hederifolium

hearts, or arrowheads.

HABIT, USE, AND GOOD COMPANIONS: Low-growing (4" to 6") plants arise from corms. Particularly good in the difficult spots around the bases of trees. Best combined with other fall-flowering bulbs such as autumn crocus *(Crocus speciosa),* autumn snowflake *(Leucojum autumnale),* or threadleaf nerine *(Nerine filifolia).* Not recommended for planting with groundcovers, which will outcompete it.

HOW TO GROW: Probably the most forgiving of the cyclamen species, and the easiest to grow, because it tolerates moisture during its period of dormancy. Must be planted in well-drained soil. Can set seed in the garden. Once fruit has formed, stems curl tightly to the ground, where capsules remain until seeds are released. Some naturally occurring seedlings may be fragrant.

CULTIVARS AND RELATED SPECIES: The culti-

DRY
SHADE

Epimedium x *versicolor* 'Sulphureum'

var 'Album' has white flowers. 'Bowles Apollo' has pink flowers, and leaves flushed pink and very heavily marbled with silver. *C. coum* flowers in winter, producing hot pink, pale pink, or white flowers with shorter, more rounded petals. It is a good candidate for clay soils with good drainage because it prefers moisture in winter while actively growing but requires summer dryness. Permanent drainage can be added to heavy clays by mixing in an inch of pea gravel or an expanded slate product.

Epimedium x *versicolor* 'Sulphureum'
BISHOP'S WORT
(Bicolor Barrenwort)
NATIVE HABITAT AND RANGE: Hybrid of *E. grandiflorum* (from Japan) and *E. pinnatum* ssp. *colchicum* (from Iran)
USDA HARDINESS ZONE: 4 to 8

OUTSTANDING FEATURES: Long sprays of pale yellow flowers appear as new foliage emerges from ground level. The flowers resemble a bishop's miter, hence the common name. Leaves are shaped like lopsided hearts and have a red flush, as though they have been embroidered with red silk. Occasionally, leaves may turn a clear red in autumn.
HABIT, USE, AND GOOD COMPANIONS: 12" to 16" tall. Grows from rhizomes and spreads 4" to 5" per year. Semi-evergreen (until a hard freeze turns the leaves to beige toast). With its mounding habit, bishop's wort is a good foil for upright plants such as ferns, Solomon's seal, woodland grasses, and Japanese sedge *(Carex morrowii)*.
HOW TO GROW: Plant divisions in fall in well-prepared, humus-enriched soil. Old leaves should be removed in very early spring so that the flowers can be seen

and appreciated. Extremely tolerant of dry shade, and will even thrive beneath the notoriously fibrous-rooted maples.

CULTIVARS AND RELATED SPECIES: *Epimedium alpinum,* originally from southern and central Europe, is very drought-tolerant. Growing 1' tall and spreading 8" to 12" a year, it makes an ideal groundcover. Small, cream-spurred flowers with red sepals are held beneath the leaves. *Epimedium* x *rubrum* (zones 4 to 8), a hybrid of *E. alpinum* and *E. grandiflorum,* is semi-evergreen with spiny-edged foliage margined and veined with red. Long, flowering stems have racemes of dainty flowers with yellow petals and crimson inner sepals surrounded by white or cream spurs; these may reach 18" in height. *E.* x *versicolor* 'Versicolor' has coppery red inner sepals. *E.* x *versicolor* 'Neosulphureum' is short and forms tight clumps; flowers are pale yellow with outer sepals tinged purple.

Euphorbia amygdaloides var. *robbiae*
WOOD SPURGE
(Mrs. Robb's Bonnet)

NATIVE HABITAT AND RANGE: Woodlands in Europe and southwestern Asia

USDA HARDINESS ZONE: 7 to 9

OUTSTANDING FEATURES: Evergreen rosettes of leathery dark green foliage. Showy bracts surrounding the flowers are yellow to chartreuse or lime-green in spring, fading to apricot and then brown.

Euphorbia amygdaloides var. *robbiae*

DRY
SHADE

HABIT, USE, AND GOOD COMPANIONS:
This rhizomatous perennial varies in height from 3" to 4" on dry sand to 1' to 2' on more fertile soils. It is a strikingly competitive, thick groundcover on nutrient-rich soils. It grows less thickly on dry sandy soils, and can be blended or mixed with ivies, Solomon's seal, Chinese ground orchid, or autumn fern.

HOW TO GROW: Plant in fall or spring in well-prepared, well-drained soil. Widely planted because of its tolerance for both shade and dry, sandy soil. However, it is much more vigorous in well-drained clay than in sand, and is much more luxuriant when nutrients are not limiting. Unfortunately, colonies of this species are subject to unexpected dieback.

CULTIVARS AND RELATED SPECIES: The cultivar *Euphorbia amygdaloides* 'Purpurea' has purple-red leaves and bright lime-green bracts. 'Rubra' has a compact habit, and leaves are flushed purple-red, particularly in winter and as new growth emerges in spring. Both cultivars are relatively short-lived in the garden, but seed about satisfactorily. *Euphorbia characias* ssp. *wulfenii* can be 4' to 6' tall when it flowers (in winter where the climate is mild and in spring elsewhere). Its evergreen foliage is blue-gray, and bract color varies from lime-green to chartreuse. Some cultivars include 'Lambrook Yellow' and 'Humpty Dumpty (a compact form). The hybrid 'Jade

Dragon' *(E. characias* ssp. *wulfenii* x *E. amygdaloides* 'Rubra') is hardy to zone 6 with protection.

Heuchera americana
AMERICAN CORAL BELLS
(Alumroot)

NATIVE HABITAT AND RANGE: Rich woods and rock outcrops throughout Eastern North America

USDA HARDINESS ZONE: 4 to 8

OUTSTANDING FEATURES: American coral bells has evergreen ruffled foliage and airy greenish flowers borne in panicles in spring. It has superb tolerance of heat and humidity.

HABIT, USE, AND GOOD COMPANIONS:
Foliage is a ground-hugging clump, but flowering stems can reach 2' to 3'. When planted near the edge of a garden, the see-through quality of its haze of small flowers adds a sense of depth. Flowering takes place between April and June, depending on the zone. Combines well with blue woodland phlox *(Phlox divaricata),* fairybells *(Disporum sessile* 'Variegatum'), primula hybrids, lesser celandine *(Ranunculus ficaria),* spring bulbs, Italian arum *(Arum italicum),* and hybrid hellebores.

HOW TO GROW: Divide in fall and plant in nutrient-rich, well-drained soil. (It can tolerate dry sandy soils with some summer watering.)

CULTIVARS AND RELATED SPECIES: There

are many hybrids of *H. americana:* 'Garnet' has green leaves deeply suffused with red in winter; 'Silver Veil' has fresh green, ruffled leaves with pronounced silver marbling; 'Velvet Night' has velvety, dark purple foliage; and 'Rain of Fire' is green with silver marbling and a pronounced red edge to the leaf in spring. 'Dale's Strain', a seed-grown strain, has green leaves overlaid with silver. The cultivar 'Montrose Ruby' is a hybrid of 'Dale's Strain' and *H. micrantha* 'Palace Purple'. It has reddish purple leaves flushed with silver. Cultivar 'Eco-magnifolia' has silver leaves with dark green edges and veins picked out in purple.

Iris tectorum
ROOF IRIS

NATIVE HABITAT AND RANGE: Open woods and scrubland in central and southwest China, naturalized in Japan

USDA HARDINESS ZONE: 4 to 8

OUTSTANDING FEATURES: Broad arching fans of medium green foliage, and large (3" to 4"), flattened, lilac-blue flowers in spring. One of the largest crested irises.

HABIT, USE, AND GOOD COMPANIONS: Height to 18" to 24" in flower. Foliage is semi-evergreen. Can be grown in combination with its smaller relative *Iris cristata* and pink-flowered *Oxalis crassipes*. Also nice in the woodland garden with

Iris tectorum

hostas, or in the shade with showy skull-cap *(Scutellaria incana)* and cream-colored *Viola striata.* Ferns, sedges, and other fine-textured plants are lovely when contrasted with the bold foliage.

HOW TO GROW: Plant the rhizomes of roof iris near the surface of humus-enriched, well-prepared soil. Clumps can be divided in fall. It can tolerate full sun but is probably a more graceful plant in shade. Plants need a half day of full sun to grow well in the North.

CULTIVARS AND RELATED SPECIES: Cultivar 'Alba' has white flowers. In cultivar 'Variegata', flowers are lilac-blue, and foliage is beautifully variegated in spring with yellow, cream, and green stripes.

make a nice background for a spring vignette of cream-colored, swan-necked daffodils, single blue cinnamon-scented Roman hyacinths, and pale yellow forms of lesser celandine *(Ranunculus ficaria)*.

HOW TO GROW: Plant in average to rich humusy soil in light to full shade. Simple to divide. May be divided in spring or fall. Replant divisions in well-drained soil enriched with organic matter. Best in evergreen shade for protection against damage to foliage during severe winters. Because it is slow to recover from being cut back, remove only the damaged foliage from the plant in the spring.

CULTIVARS AND RELATED SPECIES: The species *O. jaburan* is a larger plant (18" to 24" tall) with medium to dark green

---

Ophiopogon jaburan 'Vittatus' ('Variegatus')

VARIEGATED MONDO GRASS (Variegated White Lilyturf)

NATIVE HABITAT AND RANGE: Woods and scrubland in Asia

USDA HARDINESS ZONE: 7 to 9

OUTSTANDING FEATURES: Evergreen clumps of pale green foliage striped and edged with creamy white. Produces arching sprays of dangling small white tubular flowers in late spring or early summer.

HABIT, USE, AND GOOD COMPANIONS: Clump former to 15" tall. Can be used as a tall groundcover, an edging plant, or a specimen plant. Clumps of this cultivar

O. planiscapus 'Nigrescens'

foliage, which flowers in late spring to summer. *O. japonicus* (dwarf mondo grass) forms short (4") tufts of dark green foliage. Its stoloniferous habit makes it a good groundcover, or even a substitute for grass in shaded areas not subject to heavy foot traffic. *O. planiscapus* 'Nigrescens' (black mondo grass, zone 6 to 9) has purple-black leaves and light violet flowers. It is not aggressively stoloniferous but in time can form a thick groundcover.

P. terminalis 'Variegata'

Pachysandra stylosa
CHINESE PACHYSANDRA

NATIVE HABITAT AND RANGE: Woodlands in China or Korea

USDA HARDINESS ZONE: 5 to 8

OUTSTANDING FEATURES: Broad, sharply pointed, shiny evergreen leaves accent showy clusters of large white flowers in early spring.

HABIT, USE, AND GOOD COMPANIONS: This slow-growing stoloniferous Asian woodlander grows 6" to 8" tall. More elegant and less aggressive than its common cousin *P. terminalis,* it is better used as an accent plant than as a groundcover. Chinese pachysandra is more tolerant of heat and humidity than *P. terminalis,* and is therefore a better choice for the shade gardener in warmer zones. Combine with lacy-leaved, frothy-flowered rue anemone, ferns, black mondo grass, green-and-gold, and white-flowered epimediums.

HOW TO GROW: Plant in fall or spring in well-prepared soil enriched with humus. Divide plants in fall.

CULTIVARS AND RELATED SPECIES: *P. terminalis* (Japanese pachysandra, zones 4 to 8) is a well-known evergreen groundcover. It is strongly stoloniferous with clusters of small white flowers rising above the foliage in spring. Cultivar 'Silver Edge' has light green foliage narrowly edged in silver-white. 'Variegata' has pale green leaves with creamy white variegation and grows very slowly. 'Green Sheen' has glossy green foliage and is more tolerant of heat and humidity than the species. *P. procumbens* (Allegheny spurge) grows 8" to 12" tall. This southeastern woodlander (zones 4 to 8) prefers slightly moist soils, though established clumps are quite drought-tolerant. White, short-stalked flowers appear above the beautifully mottled, semi-evergreen foliage in early spring.

DRY
SHADE

Penstemon smallii
SMALL'S BEARDSTONGUE

NATIVE HABITAT AND RANGE: Mountain cliffs, banks, and forest edges in North Carolina, Tennessee

USDA HARDINESS ZONE: 5 to 8

OUTSTANDING FEATURES: One of the showiest southeastern penstemons, with inflorescences carrying up to 50 flowers per stem. Flowers are up to 1" long, and soft lilac in color with a purple-spotted throat. Flowers appear in spring, but if deadheaded will continue throughout the summer.

HABIT, USE, AND GOOD COMPANIONS: Leaves form a basal rosette, with flowering stems to 18" to 24". Tolerant of both shade and sun. In shade-grown plants, flowering stems arch gracefully, but in full sun stems are erect and bear flowers with a stronger red-violet hue. In winter sun, the evergreen foliage turns a beautiful burgundy color. Grows well in the shade with Japanese painted ferns, silver-leafed gingers, or ivy leafed cyclamen *(Cyclamen hederifolium)*. Excellent on banks with ivies, Solomon's seal, ferns, and green-and-gold. Like most penstemons, individual plants are short-lived, but this one readily seeds in and may spread in the garden.

HOW TO GROW: Plant in fall or spring in well-drained soil. Cut back flowering stems before seedset to encourage the production of new flowering stems throughout the summer. Allow the flowers of late summer to set seed in the fall, so that new plants can be established. This species naturally occurs in woods, on cliffs, and on roadbanks, mostly in the shade.

CULTIVARS AND RELATED SPECIES: Sandhills penstemon *(Penstemon australis)*, which flowers from May to August and inhabits sandhills, pine woods, and burned-over thickets, is also shade tolerant. Its flower color varies from rose to lavender and violet, and its basal foliage is coarsely toothed. Most other penstemons are not shade tolerant.

Polygonatum odoratum 'Variegatum'
VARIEGATED JAPANESE SOLOMON'S SEAL

NATIVE HABITAT AND RANGE: Rich woods in Europe, Asia

USDA HARDINESS ZONE: 4 to 8

OUTSTANDING FEATURES: Plants are beautiful even as they emerge from the ground in spring. Leaves are tightly furled around the stem and are white and green flushed with pink, like sticks of wintergreen candy rising out of the earth. Later, green-tipped white flowers dangle like bells beneath arching stems clothed with green leaves edged in creamy white. The variegated foliage brightens shady spots in the garden. In autumn, the foliage turns first lemon

Polygonatum odoratum 'Variegatum'

however, be transplanted at any time of the year if watered adequately until re-established. Tolerant of the driest shade, and grows well even under such trees as Bull Bay magnolia *(Magnolia grandiflora)* and willow oak *(Quercus phellos)*. It also grows exceptionally well in moist to wet shade, and in addition tolerates some sun. One of the most versatile shade plants in terms of its tolerances, and certainly one of the most beautiful.

CULTIVARS AND RELATED SPECIES: *Polygonum odoratum,* the species of which this is a cultivar, has broad, semi-glaucous green leaves on 2' stems and large fragrant flowers. It also thrives under a similar range of conditions.

yellow and then apricot before the leaves brown and wither.

HABIT, USE, AND GOOD COMPANIONS: Rhizomatous, with shoots growing to 3' and leaves up to 6" long. Bell-like flowers flaring at the tips are 1" to 1½" long. This plant's tall, arching habit makes it an ideal companion for mounding perennials such as green-and-gold, woodland phloxes, or *Pachysandra procumbens*. It also makes an attractive deciduous "skirt" for shrubs such as mountain andromeda or azaleas. Combines well in moister sites with ferns and hostas, but also excellent in dry shade with rohdeas, liriopes, and ivies.

HOW TO GROW: Divide this tough, strong colonizer in the fall. Plants can,

Rohdea japonica
JAPANESE SACRED LILY

NATIVE HABITAT AND RANGE: Woods and scrubland in Japan, southwest China

USDA HARDINESS ZONE: 6 to 10

OUTSTANDING FEATURES: Tough and beautiful with broad evergreen leaves. Sacred lily has a naked spadix which, when pollinated, produces ¾" berries. As these ripen, their color changes from green to almost translucent and shot through with gold, finally becoming a brilliant red. The ripe red fruits persist throughout the winter.

HABIT, USE, AND GOOD COMPANIONS: Broad (2½" across) leaves, 1' or more in length, rise from a central point, arranged in a loose vase shape. Wonderful structural plants for the garden. The bold foliage provides an excellent contrast to finely cut foliage of maidenhair fern or lady fern. A superb accent plant when used with low groundcovers such as variegated ivies, periwinkle, ajugas, or green-and-gold. Can also be planted with clumping plants such as gingers or tiarellas.

HOW TO GROW: Performs best if planted in well-prepared, well-drained humus-enriched soil, but will thrive in ordinary garden soil. Can flourish in deciduous shade, evergreen shade, or shade from buildings. Plants that have more than one crown can be divided in spring or fall. Collect ripe fruits when they fall. Remove the flesh, and plant seeds in the ground where new plants are desired; they will sprout by the following spring.

CULTIVARS AND RELATED SPECIES: Hundreds of cultivars exist in Japan where rohdeas are prized by collectors. 'Marginata' is taller than the species (18"), with narrow, dark green leaves edged in white, which curve from a central rosette almost to the ground. 'Miyako No Jo' has similar variegation. 'Tyokkiwna', with elegant, narrow green leaves, is lower-growing than the species.

Spigelia marilandica
MARYLAND PINKROOT

NATIVE HABITAT AND RANGE: Rich open woods throughout the southeastern U.S.

USDA HARDINESS ZONE: 4 to 9

OUTSTANDING FEATURES: Long, narrow, brilliant red flower buds open at the tip to reveal a bright chartreuse to yellow interior. Flowers are tubular, 1½" to 2" long, and appear in midsummer.

HABIT, USE, AND GOOD COMPANIONS: 15" to 18" stems clothed in narrow lance-shaped, dark green leaves. The combination of narrow foliage and tubular flowers creates a fine texture that contrasts well with large-leaved shrubs such as *Aucuba japonica* 'Gold Dust' and big-leaved perennials such as hostas, evergreen ligularias, and bergenias. Particularly striking with gold-leaved hostas. Long-lived and reliable.

HOW TO GROW: Clumps can be divided in fall and planted in well-prepared, slightly acid soil. Because it is a native of rich woods, Maryland pinkroot is best grown in soil amply enriched with humus or compost. It tolerates both dry and moist well-drained sites, and grows well in medium to light shade or at the edge of the shade garden. (In the northern part of its range, it can tolerate considerably more sun if soil is sufficiently moist.)

CULTIVARS AND RELATED SPECIES: None.

Spigelia marilandica

Stylophorum diphyllum

Stylophorum lasiocarpum
ASIAN WOOD POPPY

NATIVE HABITAT AND RANGE: Woodlands in central and eastern China

USDA HARDINESS ZONE: 4 to 9

OUTSTANDING FEATURES: This Asian counterpart to our native wood poppy distinguishes itself by its ability to tolerate much drier soils, by the soft butter-yellow color of its flowers, and its continuous flowering from spring throughout the summer, if deadheaded.

HABIT, USE, AND GOOD COMPANIONS: Clumps are 15" tall. Leaves are deciduous. Basal rosettes have bold, distinctively shaped, lyre-like notched leaves, which are slightly hairy on the surface; stems have fewer leaves and carry clusters of 1½", poppy-like, single yellow flowers at their tips. Can be grown in combination with such plants as *Helleborus* x *hybridus, Arum italicum,* heucheras, tiarellas, *Iris tectorum, Iris cristata*, and white bleeding-hearts.

HOW TO GROW: The Asian wood poppy has beautiful, peachy pink roots, which can be seen only at the time of planting. The red sap exuded from cut roots or leaves is typical of some members of the poppy family. Plant in improved loamy or clay-based soil with ample organic matter and adequate drainage. Also easy to grow from seed. The elongated seed capsules rupture and scatter seed when ripe, so harvest seed just before the capsules are completely dry.

CULTIVARS AND RELATED SPECIES: *Stylopho-*

rum diphyllum, native to North America, produces larger (2"), bright yellow, poppy-like flowers in late spring and prefers moist shade rather than dry shade. Zones 4 to 8.

COMPANION SHRUBS & TREES

Shrubs

Agarista populifolia—
Florida Leucothoe
Aucuba japonica—
Japanese Aucuba
Callicarpa americana—
American Beautyberry
*Calycanthus floridus—*Carolina Allspice
*Camellia japonica—*Japanese Camellia
Camellia sasanqua—
Sasanqua Camellia
Cephalotaxus harringtonia—
Japanese Plum Yew
Choysia ternata—
Mexican Mock Orange
*Comptonia peregrina—*Sweet Fern
Conradina verticillata—
Cumberland Rosemary
Corylopsis glabrescens—
Fragrant Winter Hazel
*Danae racemosa—*Poet's Laurel
*Daphne genkwa—*Lilac Daphne
*Daphne odora—*Winter Daphne
Deutzia crenata 'Nikko'—
Nikko Deutzia

*Diervilla sessilifolia—*Southern Bush
Honeysuckle
*Elaeagnus pungens—*Thorny Elaeagnus
Eleutherococcus sieboldianus
'Variegatus'—Five Leaf Aralia
*Gaultheria procumbens—*Wintergreen
*Holodiscus discolor—*Apache Plume
*Ilex glabra—*Inkberry
*Illicium floridanum—*Florida Anise
*Illicium henryi—*Henry Anise Tree
*Illicium parviflorum—*Small Anise Tree
*Indigofera kirilowii—*Kirilow Indigo
*Kalmia angustifolia—*Sheep Laurel
*Kalmia latifolia—*Mountain Laurel
*Kerria japonica—*Japanese Kerria
Leucothoe axillaris—
Weeping Leucothoe
*Mahonia bealei—*Chinese Grape Holly
*Mahonia japonica—*Japanese Mahonia
*Menziesia pilosa—*Minnie-Bush
Neviusia alabamensis—
Alabama Snow-wreath
*Osmanthus americanus—*Devilwood
*Osmanthus fragrans—*Tea Olive
Philadelphus lewisii—
Lewis' Mock Orange
*Pieris japonica—*Lily-of-the-valley Shrub,
Japanese Andromeda
Rhododendron catawbiense—
Catawba Rhododendron
Rhododendron 'Mary Fleming'—
'Mary Fleming' Rhododendron
Rhododendron 'PJM'—
'PJM' Rhododendron
Rhododendron 'Windbeam'—
'Windbeam' Rhododendron

DRY
SHADE

Rhododendron calendulaceum—
Flame Azalea
Rhododendron canescens—
Piedmont Azalea
Rhododendron periclymenoides—
Pinxterbloom Azalea
Rhododendron prunifolium—
Pruneleaf Azalea
Rhododendron vaseyi—
Pink Shell Azalea
Rhododendron yedoense var.
*poukhanense—*Korean Azalea
Rhododendron 'George L. Tabor'—
'George L. Tabor' Azalea
*Rhus aromatica—*Fragrant Sumac
*Ruscus aculeatus—*Butcher's Broom
*Sabal minor—*Sabal Palm
*Sarcococca hookeriana—*Sweet Box
*Sarcococca ruscifolia—*Sallau
*Skimmia japonica—*Japanese Skimmia
Symphoricarpos x *chenaultii—*
Coralberry
Ternstroemia gymnanthera—
Japanese Ternstroemia
Vaccinium crassifolium—
Creeping Blueberry
*Vaccinium stramineum—*Deerberry
*Viburnum setigerum—*Tea Viburnum
X *Fatshedera lizei—*Tree Ivy
*Yucca filamentosa—*Adam's Needle

Small Trees

Amelanchier x *grandiflora—*
Serviceberry

*Cercis canadensis—*Redbud
Chimonanthus retusus—
Chinese Fringe Tree
*Cornus florida—*Flowering Dogwood
*Cornus kousa—*Chinese Dogwood
*Hamamelis virginiana—*Witchhazel
*Ilex pedunculosa—*Longstalk Holly
*Ilex vomitoria—*Yaupon Holly
*Oxydendrum arboreum—*Sourwood
Stewartia pseudocamellia—
Japanese Stewartia
*Styrax japonica—*Japanese Snowball

Trees

Acer saccharum ssp. *nigrum—*Black
Maple
*Diospyros virginiana—*Persimmon
Gymnocladus dioicus—
Kentucky Coffeetree
*Ilex opaca—*American Holly
*Magnolia fraseri—*Fraser Magnolia
*Nyssa sylvatica—*Black Gum, Tupelo
*Quercus falcata—*Southern Red Oak
*Quercus prinus—*Chestnut Oak
*Quercus stellata—*Post Oak
*Tsuga canadensis—*Canadian Hemlock

Perennials for Moist Shade

BY C. COLSTON BURRELL

Moist shade is the kind of shade found in mesic hardwood forests, where tall trees lie bare all winter, and a cloak of rich green is rewoven at the start of each new season and shed with the return of autumn. We can learn much about gardening in the shade by tuning into this seasonal rhythm. In spring, light and moisture are abundant, and plant growth is rapid and luxuriant. As the trees leaf out, light is reduced, and plants vie with the trees for available moisture. Plants that thrive in moist soils grow near seepages, streams, and other water sources, or on floodplains where the soil does not dry out except during drought. Plants in this section will perform best where the soil is rich in humus and loam and is able to hold moisture from one rainfall to another. Supplemental watering may be necessary where the soils are lean or where root competition is great. In sites that are consistently dry in summer, try the plants recommended on the preceding pages.

FERNS, GRASSES, & SEDGES

Athyrium niponicum 'Pictum'
JAPANESE PAINTED FERN
NATIVE HABITAT AND RANGE: Moist rich

Athyrium niponicum, at left and center

woods and meadows in Japan
USDA HARDINESS ZONES: 4 to 8
OUTSTANDING FEATURES: The two-toned silver and sea-green fronds with pink stipes are sure to capture attention in the lightly shaded garden. The deep red fiddleheads and young fronds emerge in spring before the trees leaf out. Plants grow quickly into broad clumps with multiple crowns. The spring fronds are gracefully arching; the fertile fronds produced in summer are more erect.
HABIT, USE, AND GOOD COMPANIONS: This fern's spreading, luminescent vase of shimmering fronds captures both sunlight and moonlight. Use drifts to brighten up a terrace used for evening entertaining. Makes a sophisticated groundcover in a moist, lightly shaded spot.

MOIST SHADE

Perfect as an accent among the dark green foliage of gingers and hellebores, or combined with the purple leaves of *Ligularia dentata* 'Desdemona', *Heuchera* 'Plum Pudding', and *Cimicifuga simplex* 'Hillside Black Beauty', and flowers that accentuate the pink stipes.

HOW TO GROW: Plants look their best in rich soil with even moisture, and grow most vigorously in light to partial shade. They languish and are rather stunted in full shade. Plants are easily divided any time, as they produce new fronds all summer.

CULTIVARS AND RELATED SPECIES: *Athyrium filix-femina,* lady fern, is bright green and more robust, with fronds reaching 3' or more. The delicate fronds are intricately divided, creating a lacy effect in the garden. Self-sown plants are often abundant where soil is moist. Many named forms with crested and plumose fronds are available. *Athyrium otophorum,* eared lady fern, has lime-green, triangular fronds to 1' or more long, carried in an attractive, loose cluster.

Carex siderosticha 'Variegata'

Carex siderosticha 'Variegata'
VARIEGATED SEDGE

NATIVE HABITAT AND RANGE: Rich woods in eastern China, Manchuria

USDA HARDINESS ZONES: 4 to 8

OUTSTANDING FEATURES: The broad, strap-shaped leaves of this decorative sedge form tufted clumps often mistaken for a fine-textured hosta. The light green leaves are edged and streaked with creamy white. In spring, leaves are squat, but by mid-summer may reach nearly 1' long. Small flowers with ragged yellow stamens appear in early spring before the leaves emerge. The plain green wild form is seldom seen in gardens.

HABIT, USE, AND GOOD COMPANIONS: Established clumps form a bright groundcover under shrubs and flowering trees. Use them as an accent and to add light to darker foliage combinations of ferns, epimediums, and foamflowers. They are lovely when planted with white flowers such as bleeding-hearts, primroses, and phlox. A container full of this sedge on a terrace or inserted in a garden bed makes a memorable display.

HOW TO GROW: Grows best in light, humus-rich or peaty soils in light to full shade. Clumps are easily divided as they emerge in spring or in mid-summer when new shoots are produced. Slugs adore the leaves as much as gardeners do. Use beer traps or diatomaceous earth to deter them.

CULTIVARS AND RELATED SPECIES: *Carex grayi,* Gray's sedge, has medium-textured, bright green leaves in tufted clumps. The allure of this bewitching sedge lies in the mace-shaped seed clusters that crowd the foot-tall scapes throughout the summer. *Carex nigra,* black-flowered sedge, has 12" to 18", medium-textured, sea-green leaves. This creeper forms dense mats of luxurious foliage in light to full shade. The nodding flower clusters on 1' stems are black. 'Variegata' has leaves attractively edged in yellow. *Carex pennsylvanica,* Pennsylvania sedge, has fine-textured, grass-like, semi-evergreen leaves carried in dense, tufted clumps. This plant is an easy-care lawn substitute in the moist or dry shade of mature trees.

Diplazium pycnocarpon
GLADE FERN

NATIVE HABITAT AND RANGE: Rich, open woods and glades in limy soils in eastern and central North America

USDA HARDINESS ZONES: 4 to 8

OUTSTANDING FEATURES: The once-divided, rich green fronds have a tropical luxuriance reminiscent of a Boston fern. Plants form multi-crowned clumps of arching, sterile leaves in spring and early summer. In late summer, the stiff, ladder-like fertile fronds are produced, some as tall as 3' or more. This fern always looks lush and attractive during the growing season, and the fronds turn yellow in the autumn.

HABIT, USE, AND GOOD COMPANIONS: Plants have slow-creeping, branched rhizomes with tightly congested fronds 1' to 3' tall. The apple-green fronds are an effusive foil for wildflowers such as Virginia bluebells, bugbane, bellwort, and trilliums. They also combine well with other ferns whose more dissected fronds form a dramatic contrast. Use a generous drift in a low spot or along the banks of a stream with umbrella leaf, phlox, and Solomon's plume.

HOW TO GROW: Plants require near neutral to limy soils, rich in humus, that are never allowed to go completely dry. Growth is most luxuriant in bright light, but plants will also grow in full shade. The delicate fronds are fragile and easily broken. Plant them in a spot protected from harsh winds. Divide the branching rhizomes as plants go dormant in autumn.

CULTIVARS AND RELATED SPECIES: *Deparia acrostichoides,* silvery spleenwort, has a similar habit, but the fronds are twice-divided and sea-green. This species is often overlooked because the fronds resemble other ferns. The 2' to 3' fronds turn straw-colored in autumn.

MOIST
SHADE

MOIST SHADE

Phegopteris (Thelypteris) hexa-gonoptera
SOUTHERN BEECH FERN

NATIVE HABITAT AND RANGE: Moist rich woods in eastern and central North America

USDA HARDINESS ZONES: 4 to 9

OUTSTANDING FEATURES: Broad, triangular fronds are gathered in open clusters 1' to 2' tall. The fronds are held upright or horizontally, creating an attractive, rich green groundcover. The fertile and sterile fronds are similar in appearance. They turn pale yellow in autumn.

HABIT, USE, AND GOOD COMPANIONS: Plants grow from a creeping rhizome, so the fronds are arrayed in lines or loose clusters. This fern thrives among the roots of trees and shrubs where few other plants prosper. Use it as part of a groundcover tapestry of wildflowers with persistent foliage such as foamflowers, bishop's hat, wild gingers, and other ferns.

HOW TO GROW: Plant in rich, moist acidic soils in light to full shade. In very rich soil with ample light, the plants form dense, tangled clumps. In shadier sites, the fronds are more widely spaced, so you can appreciate their individual forms. In the wild, these tough ferns grow among the roots of mature beech trees in dense, dry shade. Plants are easily divided in spring or autumn.

CULTIVARS AND RELATED SPECIES: *Phegopteris connectilis,* northern beech fern, has narrower fronds that face outward. The lowest pinnae or leaflets are bent backwards, resembling the ears of a startled rabbit. The bright green fronds all face the same direction, making an attractive display, especially on a slope. This plant is hardier, to zone 3, but less tolerant of summer heat.

FLOWERING PLANTS

Anemone nemorosa
EUROPEAN WOOD ANEMONE

NATIVE HABITAT AND RANGE: Open woods and meadows of Europe

USDA HARDINESS ZONES: 3 to 8

OUTSTANDING FEATURES: Like a starry galaxy fallen to earth, the snow-white flowers of this diminutive plant are

Anemone nemorosa

borne in profusion atop the broad clumps of foliage in early spring. Only one flower is carried on each plant, but the densely packed stems assure a fabulous display. The flowers persist for several weeks. The three leaves borne in a whorl have 3 to 5 leaflets each.

HABIT, USE, AND GOOD COMPANIONS: This woodlander emerges early, when sun is plentiful. Soon after flowering, the leaves begin to wither and the plant passes quickly into dormancy. Plant among persistent wildflowers and ferns that will fill the void when they disappear for the season. Maidenhair fern, epimediums, wild gingers, foamflowers, and shooting stars are good companions.

HOW TO GROW: Plant in moist, humus-rich soil where spring sun is plentiful (shade and a lack of moisture are not a problem after the plants go dormant). Plants spread quickly from brittle rhizomes that creep just below the soil surface. In time, the rhizomes can get quite tangled, compromising the bloom. Divide plants as the foliage begins to turn yellow.

CULTIVARS AND RELATED SPECIES: 'Vestal' is a pure white, double form. 'Allenii' has light blue-purple flowers on robust plants. 'Bowle's Purple' has rich lilac flowers. *Anemone quinquefolia,* wind-flower, is native to acidic or neutral woods in North America. Less robust than its European cousin, this plant is also more difficult to establish. *Anemone*

ranunculoides, buttercup anemone, has bright buttercup-yellow flowers above a whorl of three leaves with narrow, toothed leaflets. A double form is sometimes available. *Anemonopsis macrophylla,* anemonopsis, is a distant but attractive relative with drooping, 2', branched clusters of rose-pink flowers in late summer. The divided foliage emerges early in the season, and persists through the blooming period.

Actaea pachypoda

Actaea pachypoda
WHITE BANEBERRY

NATIVE HABITAT AND RANGE: Rich woodlands and shaded roadsides in the northern portions of eastern and central North America

USDA HARDINESS ZONES: 3 to 8

MOIST
SHADE

OUTSTANDING FEATURES: Both its flowers and its fruits distinguish this native wildflower. A dense cluster of fuzzy, petalless white flowers is carried above the emerging leaves in spring. The intricately dissected leaves, borne one to a stem, may reach 1' or more across. In autumn, the elongated clusters of white fruits, each with a blue dot at the tip, resemble porcelain doll's eyes on bright carmine red stalks. Birds love the berries, but they are poisonous to people!

HABIT, USE, AND GOOD COMPANIONS: Plants produce multi-stemmed, open clumps from 1' to 3' tall. Mature plants have the appearance of small shrubs, and can be used accordingly; surround them with lower perennials and ferns. They add a strong architectural accent, especially when backlit. Use them as a focal point at the end of a path or the bend in a woodland trail. Celandine poppy, wild ginger, wild bleeding-heart, blue phlox, and wreath goldenrod are good companions.

HOW TO GROW: Plant in rich, moist, acidic or near neutral soil in light to full shade. Dense fibrous-rooted clumps can be divided in autumn with the aid of a sharp knife. Sow seeds outdoors in autumn, after removing the fleshy pulp.

CULTIVARS AND RELATED SPECIES: *Actaea rubra,* red baneberry, has dense clusters of shiny scarlet berries in late summer. The leaflets are similar but broader and flattened. Plants prefer acidic soils.

Plants are as hardy as white baneberry but less heat-tolerant. The form *neglecta* has white berries.

Aralia racemosa
SPIKENARD

NATIVE HABITAT AND RANGE: Rich deciduous or coniferous woods from the Rocky Mountains eastward

USDA HARDINESS ZONES: 3 to 8

OUTSTANDING FEATURES: The huge, divided leaves have dozens of broad, heart-shaped leaflets. The 4' to 6' plants may boast half a dozen leaves, each 3' to 4' across. The terminal clusters of small green flowers ripen into 2' clusters of purple berries in late summer. In all respects, this giant is a showstopper.

HABIT, USE, AND GOOD COMPANIONS: These large plants, though herbaceous, take up the same space as a shrub. Give them plenty of room, as a specimen or focal point, singly or in small groups. Use them among ferns, Solomon's seal, toad lilies, and wood aster to give summer privacy to a terrace or to divide spaces in the garden. New growth emerges late in spring, so the huge space left for this plant can be filled with early-blooming bulbs and wildflowers that go dormant after flowering. Spikenard is a natural bird feeder; as the berries ripen, dozens of birds will visit.

HOW TO GROW: Plant in humus-rich, acidic, or limy soils in light to dense shade. This plant even puts on a stunning show in the dense, dry shade of evergreens. Established plants have huge fleshy roots that are not easily divided, but self-sown seedlings are common.

CULTIVARS AND RELATED SPECIES: *Aralia cashemirica,* Kashmir aralia, is even bigger than spikenard. Mature clumps may be 8' or more across. The plant has a more refined look, with less divided leaves and regularly spaced leaflets. The fruits are borne in elongated clusters with ball-like bunches of deep purple berries. *Aralia cordata,* Japanese aralia, is similar to spikenard, but the stems are less erect and the flowers are carried in both terminal clusters and in the joints of the stem where the leaves emerge.

Cimicifuga simplex
AUTUMN BUGBANE

NATIVE HABITAT AND RANGE: Rich woodlands in temperate Asia

USDA HARDINESS ZONES: 3 to 8

OUTSTANDING FEATURES: The sweetly fragrant white autumn flowers open just as the season is winding down, giving the gardener a reprieve from the bloomlessness of late autumn. In northern regions, the plants may be nipped by frost while still in flower. The tall, shepherd's crook flower spikes are carried on 3' to 6' stems well above the foliage.

Cimicifuga simplex 'White Pearl'

The leaves are highly dissected into small, toothed leaflets.

HABIT, USE, AND GOOD COMPANIONS: Plants form upright, multistemmed clumps, perfect as accents or specimens, or to add height to mixed plantings of wildflowers, perennials, and ferns. They can be used in formal borders or informal situations with wood ferns, toad lilies, hellebores, ligularias, and sedges.

HOW TO GROW: Plant in rich, evenly moist soil in light to full shade. In dry soil and where nights are hot, plants shed their lower leaves in summer or early autumn; plants perform best where nights are cool. The thick, fibrous-rooted crowns have eyes like peonies, and can be divided with a sharp

MOIST
SHADE

MOIST
SHADE

knife in spring or after flowering.
CULTIVARS AND RELATED SPECIES: 'White Pearl' has snow-white flowers on 2' to 4' stalks. *C. simplex* 'Atropurpurea' has purple leaves that fade to dark green-brown in summer heat. 'Hillside Black Beauty' has purple leaves that hold their color all season. Several garden-worthy species of bugbanes are beginning to be available in the trade. Among easily obtained species is *Cimicifuga japonica,* Japanese bugbane; each leaf has three broad, shiny leaflets. Mature specimens of this dramatic, bold-textured plant are very striking. The slender, erect flower spikes are carried in late summer and autumn. *Cimicifuga racemosa,* black cohosh, is a familiar eastern wildflower with divided leaves and 4' to 6' cande-labra spikes of white flowers in early summer.

Dentaria (Cardamine) laciniata
TOOTHWORT
NATIVE HABITAT AND RANGE: Moist woods and floodplains in eastern and central North America
USDA HARDINESS ZONES: 4 to 8
OUTSTANDING FEATURES: The drooping, 4-petaled white or pale pink flowers look like small teeth, hence the common name. The flowers are carried above a whorl of three deeply dissected leaves with finger-like leaflets. They form dense colonies loaded with flowers. The foliage

Dentaria (Cardamine) laciniata

is quite variable from colony to colony.
HABIT, USE, AND GOOD COMPANIONS: Tooth-wort spreads from brittle creeping rhi-zomes to form large colonies. The plants disappear entirely after flowering, so take care not to dig into them. The rhizomes are edible, but are much love-lier in the garden than in the gullet. Combine with persistent plants such as sedges, hostas, wild gingers, and ferns that fill the void.
HOW TO GROW: Plant in rich, moist soil in spring sun or light shade. After dorman-cy, the soil can become dry, and shade is irrelevant. Divide the rhizomes as plants turn yellow. Self-sown seedlings will appear.
CULTIVARS AND RELATED SPECIES: *Dentaria*

diphylla, crinkleroot, is an ephemeral wildflower that forms a temporary groundcover of leaves divided into 3 leaflets. The open clusters of 4-petaled white to pale pink flowers are borne as the leaves are expanding. *Dentaria heptaphylla* is a choice toothwort just becoming available in the U.S. Plants have pinnate, 8-lobed leaves that set off the clusters of ¾", snow-white flowers. *Dentaria pentaphyllos* resembles toothwort but is more robust, with dramatic, 5-lobed starry leaves and 1", clear pink, nodding flowers.

Diphylleia cymosa
UMBRELLA LEAF

NATIVE HABITAT AND RANGE: Moist, cool woods in the southern Appalachian Mountains

USDA HARDINESS ZONES: 4 to 7

OUTSTANDING FEATURES: There is bold texture in the moist shade garden without hosta! The large, deeply cut leaves of this flamboyant plant have dramatic, sharply pointed lobes. In spring, small clusters of white flowers are carried above a gorgeous mound of mouth-watering foliage. The flowers give way to royal blue berries on carmine stalks. Wow.

HABIT, USE, AND GOOD COMPANIONS: This shrubby plant is a must for any garden with a flare for the dramatic. Use a generous grouping of umbrella leaf as an accent against a wall or as a focal point in a sea of fine-textured ferns and wildflowers. Mass plantings in combination with ferns mimic the way this plant grows in the wild, and are quite eye-catching. Choose fairybells, Virginia bluebell, wild geranium, epimediums, and maidenhair fern as companions.

HOW TO GROW: Plant in humus-rich, evenly moist but not soggy soil in partial to full shade. Hot sun will scorch the leaves and ruin the display for the season. Plants are hardy to zone 4, but mulch the crowns well to protect them from bitter cold. Plants seldom need division, but can be divided in spring or autumn; leave at least one large eye per division. Sow seeds outdoors as soon as they ripen, after removing the pulp.

CULTIVARS AND RELATED SPECIES: The Japanese species *Diphylleia grayii* is seldom available but garden-worthy.

Diphylleia cymosa

MOIST
SHADE

Disporum flavum
YELLOW FAIRYBELLS

NATIVE HABITAT AND RANGE: Moist woodlands in Korea and China

USDA HARDINESS ZONES: 3 to 8

OUTSTANDING FEATURES: Tall, slender, leafy stalks are crowned with drooping clusters of yellow, bell-shaped flowers in spring. The flowers peek demurely from the unfurling leaves at first, then dangle shamelessly in plain view as they mature. The lush, medium green, pleated leaves are tidy all summer, and turn russet in autumn.

HABIT, USE, AND GOOD COMPANIONS: This plant's vertical form gives lift to low plantings and becomes an accent among fine-textured ferns and meadow rues. The upright, vase-shaped clumps leave lots of room around their ankles for shorter plants such as wild gingers, bishop's hat, foamflowers, sedges, and small ferns.

HOW TO GROW: Give plants rich, humusy soil that stays moist all season. They thrive in good light, but tolerate dense shade; are slow to spread, but in time form broad, multi-stemmed clumps that are quite spectacular. Divide the creeping, horizontal rhizomes in late summer.

CULTIVARS AND RELATED SPECIES: *Disporum hookeri,* Hooker's mandarin, has branched, spreading stems clothed in pointed leaves and nodding, open, purple-spotted white bells. An orange berry forms in autumn. *Disporum lanuginosum,* nodding mandarin, has deep green flowers and lush, pointed, egg-shaped leaves. This is a rapid increaser and forms broad clumps that resemble a well-behaved bamboo. *Disporum smithii,* white fairybells, has arching branches with deep green, pleated leaves and terminal clusters of showy white flowers. The oval berries are red-orange.

Epimedium grandiflorum
BISHOP'S HAT

NATIVE HABITAT AND RANGE: Woodlands and moist rock outcroppings in Japan

USDA HARDINESS ZONES: 4 to 8

OUTSTANDING FEATURES: The delicate, 1" spurred flowers of this enchanting plant hang in loose clusters mingled with or just above the new spring foliage. Though the flowers of any one plant last barely a week, there are many clones with different colors and bloom times. The new foliage is often tinted red. Mounded clumps of divided, deciduous to semi-evergreen leaves remain neat and attractive all season.

HABIT, USE, AND GOOD COMPANIONS: The slow-spreading clumps are wider than tall, making an effective and distinctive groundcover. Several plants set out together will soon fill in to make a solid carpet. The intricately divided leaves have leathery, medium-textured leaflets. Plant them under shrubs and flowering

Epimedium grandiflorum 'Rose Queen'

trees or around rocks in the company of ferns, anemones, sedges, and ephemeral wildflowers.

HOW TO GROW: Plant in humus-rich soil in light to full shade. Established plants tolerate dry soil. Divide plants in late spring or summer, after the new growth is fully hardened. Self-sown seedlings may appear.

CULTIVARS AND RELATED SPECIES: 'Lilafee' has bicolored rose-purple flowers. 'Orion' has very large, deep rose flowers. 'Rose Queen' has large, rich rose flowers. 'White Queen' has small white flowers. Several other exquisite epimediums are becoming widely available. *Epimedium grandiflorum* var. *coreanum* is more upright, with larger leaflets and large yellow flowers held below the leaves.

Epimedium x *youngianum* is a hybrid with neat clumps of foliage and delicate leaflets. The flowers lack conspicuous spurs. 'Roseum' has rose-pink flowers. 'Niveum' is snow white.

Helleborus orientalis
LENTEN ROSE

NATIVE HABITAT AND RANGE: Moist, rocky woods in Eastern Europe

USDA HARDINESS ZONES: 4 to 9

OUTSTANDING FEATURES: The shy chalices of Lenten rose nod in open clusters from 1' stalks in late winter and early spring. The flowers, made up of showy sepals, have substantial texture and last for a month or more. As they age, they turn green. The rich, leathery, ever-

MOIST
SHADE

Helleborus orientalis

green leaves are deeply divided into elongated oval lobes. Long after the flowers have faded, the leaves grace the garden, standing through summer heat and winter snow.

HABIT, USE, AND GOOD COMPANIONS: The flowers emerge from the center of the old clump, overtopping the flattened foliage from the previous season. Many gardeners remove the old foliage as the new flowers are emerging. As the flowers fade to green, the new foliage expands, overtopping the flowering scapes, which eventually wither. Plants form crowded batches of stiff leaves from a thick, fibrous-rooted crown. Use as a groundcover under shrubs and trees, or in formal and informal gardens in combination with ferns, bulbs, and wildflowers such as foamflowers, Virginia bluebell, and wild gingers.

HOW TO GROW: Plant in moist, humus-rich soil in light to full shade. Plants form great clumps but seldom need division, except for propagation. Self-sown seedlings will be plentiful, with some variation in flower color.

CULTIVARS AND RELATED SPECIES: *Helleborus foetidus,* stinking hellebore, has tall stems to 2' with spidery, deep green leaves and terminal clusters of lime-green, bell-shaped flowers. *Helleborus niger,* Christmas rose, is beloved for its white winter flowers resembling 2" stars, carried in a tight cluster at the center of last year's leaves. Plants prefer near-neutral soil.

Helleborus purpurascens has massive, umbrella-like leaves and early, nodding green flowers flushed with purple.

Jeffersonia diphylla
TWINLEAF

NATIVE HABITAT AND RANGE: Moist, rich deciduous woods in eastern and central North America

USDA HARDINESS ZONES: 4 to 8

OUTSTANDING FEATURES: The paired leaflets that give this plant its name look like the wings of a sea-green luna moth. Snowy white flowers resembling bloodroot open in spring, but are so ephemeral they may last but a day or two. A curious, pipe-shaped seed pod forms in late spring. Upon ripening, it ejects its seeds like a cannon.

HABIT, USE, AND GOOD COMPANIONS: Plants form dense clumps of exotic-looking leaves from fibrous-rooted crowns. The leaves may reach 18" or more in height. Use them to add height to low carpets of ephemeral species such as anemones, spring beauty, and Dutchman's breeches. The leaves will fill the gaps left as the lower plants go dormant. Combine them with ferns.

HOW TO GROW: Plant in moist, humus-rich, limy soil; this plant will not thrive in acidic soils. In nature, plants are found on or near talus slopes, so they benefit from limestone rubble in the soil, especially where conditions are naturally

MOIST
SHADE

MOIST
SHADE

Jeffersonia diphylla

acidic. Large clumps are desirable and slow to mature, but they can be divided for propagation after flowering or in the autumn. Self-sown seedlings will appear. CULTIVARS AND RELATED SPECIES: *Jeffersonia dubia,* Japanese twinleaf, is more diminutive, to 1', with shield-shaped leaves and a profusion of lavender flowers produced over a week or more. This plant self-sows profusely where conditions are to its liking.

Meehania cordata
CREEPING WOOD MINT

NATIVE HABITAT AND RANGE: Rich deciduous woods in the Midwest and northern Appalachian Mountains

USDA HARDINESS ZONES: 4 to 8

OUTSTANDING FEATURES: Creeping wood mint is one of the best kept secrets among native groundcovers. The trailing stems are clothed in scalloped, rounded leaves. In spring, the new growth is studded with 1", medium blue, tubular flowers in dense clusters. The entire plant is prostrate, seldom rising more than a few inches off the ground.

HABIT, USE, AND GOOD COMPANIONS: Perfect as an open groundcover under flowering shrubs, or at the front of a bed along a woodland trail. The stems weave among other plants and are never invasive. The bright flowers come in late spring when other woodland plants are past flowering. Combine them with ferns, bleeding-hearts, bugbanes, fairybells, and other upright plants.

HOW TO GROW: Plant in moist, rich soil in light to full shade. Plants are slow to establish, and will take a few years before they settle in and start to run. Cuttings root easily in early summer, and rooted stems can be removed from the parent plant any time.

CULTIVARS AND RELATED SPECIES: *Meehania urticifolia,* an Asian woodlander, is larger and much more vigorous. Plants form 1' clumps with trailing stems. The purple-blue flowers are sometimes hidden by the luxuriant foliage.

Mertensia virginica
VIRGINIA BLUEBELL

NATIVE HABITAT AND RANGE: Moist, rich woods and floodplains in eastern and central North America

USDA HARDINESS ZONES: 4 to 9

OUTSTANDING FEATURES: The nodding, sky-blue bells of this widespread native wildflower have endeared it to gardeners since colonial times. This plant is grown in shady gardens on both sides of the Atlantic. The fresh spring shoots are deep purple. Flowers open from pink buds as soon as the 1' to 2' stalks begin to emerge in spring. The egg-shaped leaves are sea-green and decrease in size as they ascend the stem. Plants go dormant soon after flowering.

HABIT, USE, AND GOOD COMPANIONS: Multistemmed clumps form hazy blue drifts, creating a river of blue amongst bulbs, other wildflowers, and ferns. Let them seed among lawn grasses. If you delay mowing until the foliage ripens, an enchanting effect is created in the dull sameness of turfgrass. A favored combination is bluebells with white daffodils.

HOW TO GROW: Plant in moist, rich soil in full sun to light spring shade. Sites can become quite shaded after plants go dormant. Self-sown seedlings are plentiful.

Mertensia virginica

CULTIVARS AND RELATED SPECIES: *Mertensia ciliata,* lungwort, is a large plant with proportionately small flowers, but is charming nonetheless. The gray-green leaves set off the flowers. This plant is native to the western mountains. *Merten-*

sia paniculata, tall lungwort, is more delicate, with pleated leaves and tall stalks crowned by ¾" flowers in late spring. Plants are more northern in distribution and do not thrive where nights are hot.

Peltoboykinia watanabei
PELTOBOYKINIA

NATIVE HABITAT AND RANGE: Moist to wet woods in Japan

USDA HARDINESS ZONES: 4 to 8

OUTSTANDING FEATURES: The dramatic, 10" leaves resemble coarsely toothed buzz-saw blades. They are rounded with deep, sharp-pointed lobes. Few plants have such a dramatic flair. More curious than beautiful, the green, funnel-shaped flowers are carried in open, branched clusters in summer. The foliage turns clear yellow in autumn.

HABIT, USE, AND GOOD COMPANIONS: Plants form low, mounded clumps to 18" high that add a bold accent singularly or in drifts. Surround them with fine-textured ephemerals such as spring beauty and toothwort, as well as persistent ferns and sedges. Use them in masses under flowering shrubs or as a dramatic exclamation point to liven up a bland ground-cover of periwinkle or ajuga.

HOW TO GROW: Plant in humus-rich, moist to damp soil in light to full shade. The leaves will scorch if soil becomes too dry in summer. Plants form broad clumps from fibrous-rooted crowns.

Self-sown seedlings will appear.

CULTIVARS AND RELATED SPECIES: *Boykinia aconitifolia,* swamp saxifrage, is native to soggy streamsides in the Appalachians but adapts well to moist, rich garden soil. The pleated, round leaves are often edged with deep red. Flattened clusters of white flowers are produced on 1' stems. *Boykinia major,* native to western North America, is similar but overall larger in foliage and flower. Plants reach 2' tall. *Peltoboykinia tellimoides* has rounded leaves, less deeply toothed, and white flowers in open clusters. Plants grow 1' to 2' tall.

Phlox divaricata

Phlox stolonifera
CREEPING PHLOX

NATIVE HABITAT AND RANGE: Open woods, roadside embankments, and rocky slopes in the eastern U.S.

USDA HARDINESS ZONES: 3 to 8

OUTSTANDING FEATURES: Prostrate mats of creeping stems sporting pairs of rounded leaves make an attractive groundcover. In spring, 4" to 6" stalks are crowned with a whorl of tubular, flat-faced flowers. Named cultivars provide a range of colors in white, pinks, blues, and purples to satisfy every taste. The flower stalks wither after flowering, exposing the carpet of leaves beneath.

HABIT, USE, AND GOOD COMPANIONS: As a flowering groundcover, this plant has few equals. The mats are smothered with flowers in spring. Use them under shrubs and trees, or along pathways, in front of taller plants such as bishop's hat, wild bleeding heart, Allegheny spurge, trilliums, fairybells, and ferns.

HOW TO GROW: Plant in rich, moist soil in light to full shade. Plants will not bloom heavily in dense shade. Take cuttings from the trailing stems in early summer, or separate rooted portions of stem any time during the growing season.

CULTIVARS AND RELATED SPECIES: 'Blue Ridge' has lavender-blue flowers. 'Bruce's White' has white flowers with an orange eye. 'Pink Ridge' has bright purple flowers. 'Porter's Purple' has deep purple flowers. 'Sherwood Purple' has light purple flowers. *Phlox divaricata,* wild sweet William, has sweet-scented, sky-blue flowers in tight, rounded clusters on 1' stalks. The evergreen basal leaves are oval, and make a nice clump after the flowering stems wither.

'Clouds of Perfume' has strongly scented blooms. 'Dirigo Ice' has powder-blue flowers. 'Fuller's White' has pure white flowers.

Primula sieboldii

Primula sieboldii
SIEBOLD PRIMROSE

NATIVE HABITAT AND RANGE: Moist woods and wet meadows in Japan, Korea, and China

USDA HARDINESS ZONES: 3 to 8

OUTSTANDING FEATURES: The delicate clusters of pink, 5-petaled flowers are among the loveliest of the primroses. The oval, toothed leaves are attractively quilted. Plants form broad clumps covered in an abundance of 6" to 8" flower

MOIST **SHADE**

stalks. There are many flower forms, from notched to deeply fringed, and colors vary from white and pink to rose, lavender, near purple, and near red. Many named selections are available. In Japan, there is a mania for this beloved wildflower in all its forms.

HABIT, USE, AND GOOD COMPANIONS: Catch it while you can. This lovely plant emerges in spring and soon covers itself with showy pink flowers nearly an inch across. After a month of bloom, it slips quietly into dormancy. Combine it with bulbs, bleeding hearts, phlox, hellebores, and ferns. Plant them around late-emerging hostas and aralias; as the plants go dormant, the hosta leaves will cover the bare spot.

HOW TO GROW: Plant in humus-rich soil, moist or wet in spring, drier in summer when plants go dormant. Spreads by shallow, brittle rhizomes that can be divided as the foliage yellows. Self-sown seedling may appear.

CULTIVARS AND RELATED SPECIES: *Primula cortusoides* is similar but has smaller pink flowers in a tight cluster on 8" to 10" stalks. *Primula kisoana,* woodland primrose, has toothed, fan-shaped leaves that are lush and felted. The deep rose or white flowers are carried in open clusters on 4" to 6" stems. Spreads underground to form broad, open colonies.

Salvia koyamae
WOODLAND SAGE

NATIVE HABITAT AND RANGE: Open woodlands in Japan

USDA HARDINESS ZONES: 4, with protection, to 9

OUTSTANDING FEATURES: A sage that blooms like gangbusters in the shade? That's right. This attractive plant has deep green, felted arrow-head leaves on 1' stalks. The foliage adds texture to the spring and summer garden. Plants flower in late summer. The terminal clusters of ¾" yellow flowers are an added bonus. The unique color makes it doubly attractive. Plants bloom for several months, carrying the garden into autumn. In my zone 4 garden, plants have never bloomed, but the foliage is asset enough for me to keep it.

HABIT, USE, AND GOOD COMPANIONS: Plants spread by trailing runners to form broad, open clumps. They are lovely combined with purple flowered tricyrtis, turtleheads, sedges, and fine-textured ferns. Use them as a groundcover under shrubs and trees.

HOW TO GROW: Plant in humus-rich, moist soil in light to full shade. Plants bloom best with some sun, but do not like full sun, especially in warmer zones. Established clumps tolerate dry soil.

CULTIVARS AND RELATED SPECIES: *Salvia glutinosa* is similar but a bit taller and more open in form. This plant is not yet widely available in this country. Hardy to zone 6. *Salvia lyrata,* lyre-leaf sage, is considered a weed by some, but butterflies love the flowers. The basal leaves are constricted in the middle. The 1" stalks bear pale blue flowers from spring through the summer. A form with purple leaves is available.

Solidago caesia

Solidago caesia
WREATH GOLDENROD

NATIVE HABITAT AND RANGE: Open woods, woodland borders, and rocky slopes in eastern and central North America

USDA HARDINESS ZONES: 4 to 9

OUTSTANDING FEATURES: Wreath goldenrod is one of many woodland species that are excellent garden plants. The 2" to 3" stalks are clothed in lance-shaped, blue-green leaves that grow smaller toward the top of the stalk, and intermingle with the flowers. The bright, lemon-yellow flowers form terminal wands that begin in the leaf axils.

HABIT, USE, AND GOOD COMPANIONS: Forms dense, beautifully textured foliage clumps from slow-creeping rhizomes. The flowers add light to shaded recesses long dulled by summer's dog days. Combine them with toadlilies, woodland asters, colchicums, turtleheads, and ferns.

HOW TO GROW: Plant in moist, average to rich soil in light to full shade. Plants are more vigorous and heavily flowered with some direct sun, but will bloom even in dense shade. Easily grown from stem cuttings taken in early summer, or by division.

CULTIVARS AND RELATED SPECIES: *Solidago bicolor,* silverrod, has silvery white flowers in dense, slender, wand-like spikes in late summer. Tolerates dry soil and dense shade. *Solidago flexicaulis,* zig-zag goldenrod, has tall stems to 3' that bend back and forth between the nodes of the opposite leaves, creating a zig-zag pattern. The rounded, sharply toothed leaves decrease in size as they ascend the stem, intermingling with the wand-like terminal clusters of yellow flowers. Plants bloom in late summer and autumn. Hardy to zone 3.

MOIST
SHADE

MOIST SHADE

Tiarella cordifolia var. *collina*

Tiarella cordifolia
ALLEGHENY FOAMFLOWER

NATIVE HABITAT AND RANGE: Moist woods and rocky slopes in eastern North America

USDA HARDINESS ZONES: 3 to 8

OUTSTANDING FEATURES: Shiny, evergreen foliage and fountains of frothy white flowers in spring make foamflower one of the most attractive and versatile spring wildflowers. The 6" to 8" spikes of tiny, starry flowers are densely packed into cylindrical clusters. The triangular, 3-lobed leaves are soft and hairy and are produced in open clumps and along the trailing stems.

HABIT, USE, AND GOOD COMPANIONS: Unsurpassed as a flowering groundcover under flowering shrubs and trees and among shallow-rooted shade trees. Lovely when accented with taller

baneberries, bluebells, Solomon's seal, fairybells, and ferns. Fall crocus are lovely against the background of purple-tinted fall foliage.

HOW TO GROW: Plant in humus-rich, evenly moist soil in light to full shade. Plants romp all over the garden, and will overpower their neighbors if given half a chance. Sever rooted runners for propagation, or sow fresh seed indoors on a fine-textured seedling mix.

CULTIVARS AND RELATED SPECIES: *T. polyphylla* 'Running Tapestry' has somewhat triangular leaves with deep red central veins. 'Slick Rock' is a diminutive trailer with 2", sharply lobed leaves. *Tiarella cordifolia* var. *collina (T. wherryi)* is similar, but forms discrete clumps of foliage and flowers and does not run. This plant is often quite showy in bloom, as the flowers are gathered together at the center of the foliage clumps. In some clones, the flowers have a pink tint. 'Oakleaf' has deeply cut leaves with rounded lobes. 'Tiger Stripe' is similar, with central red veins. *Tellima grandiflora,* fringecups, native to the Pacific Northwest, has rounded leaves resembling a coral bell. Tall slender spikes of ornately fringed cup-shaped flowers are produced in late spring.

Tricyrtis hirta
TOAD LILY

NATIVE HABITAT AND RANGE: Moist rocky

MOIST
SHADE

Tricyrtis latifolia

MOIST SHADE

woods and outcroppings in Japan

USDA HARDINESS ZONES: 4 to 8

OUTSTANDING FEATURES: Arching stems 2' to 3' tall are clothed with pairs of hairy, lanceolate leaves resembling an angel-wing begonia. In autumn, axillary clusters of 1", purple-spotted white or pink flowers open in one-sided rows on top of the vase of arching stems. The odd, 6-petaled flowers, often likened to orchids, are saucer-shaped, and have a protruding central column that bears the reproductive structures. In northern climates, killing frost may take the stems just as flowering begins. When cold weather is forecast, cut the stems and bring them indoors for weeks of enjoyment.

HABIT, USE, AND GOOD COMPANIONS: Spreads slowly by short runners to form multistemmed clumps that are stunning in flower. Plant them with late bloomers such as colchicums, wreath goldenrod, and white woodland aster, and bright berries such as baneberry and blue cohosh. Fruiting shrubs such as beautyberry and deciduous hollies are attractive companions.

HOW TO GROW: Plant in moist, humus-rich soil in light to full shade. In dry years, the foliage may be yellowing or browning off by the time the flowers open. Divide the spreading clumps in spring or after flowering.

CULTIVARS AND RELATED SPECIES: *Tricyrtis formosana* is an upright species that has pleated oval leaves and lavender flowers with violet speckles in late summer and early autumn. *Tricyrtis latifolia,* yellow toad lily, has upward-facing yellow flowers speckled with purple in summer. This is a good choice in northern regions where frost comes early. *Tricyrtis macranthopsis* has drooping stems clothed in glossy, pleated leaves and 1", rich yellow, tubular flowers that hang from the leaf axils in late autumn. A mature specimen is a dramatic sight.

Trillium grandiflorum
LARGE-FLOWERED TRILLIUM

NATIVE HABITAT AND RANGE: Rich deciduous woods and floodplains in eastern and central North America

USDA HARDINESS ZONES: 3 to 9

OUTSTANDING FEATURES: Pure white, 3-petaled flowers up to 3" across are held erect or outfacing above a whorl of bright green leaves on 18" stalks. Each plant produces a single flower. This is the showiest of the trillium species, beloved by temperate-climate gardeners everywhere.

HABIT, USE, AND GOOD COMPANIONS: Plants produce single or paired stalks from fleshy rhizomes. In time, self-sown seedlings will form floriferous, showy groups along woodland walks and in shaded beds. Combine them with blue phlox, bleeding hearts, wild gingers, bishop's hat, bellworts, and ferns.

HOW TO GROW: Plant in rich, moist soil in

Trillium grandiflorum

MOIST
SHADE

light to full shade. Plants need full sun in spring before the trees leaf out to flower freely; plants will languish in deep, year-round shade. Sow fresh seed outdoors. Seedlings take 7 years to grow to flowering size. Many trilliums are still collected from the wild for sale in nurseries. Buy only *nursery propagated* plants—and be aware that *nursery grown* does *not* mean the same thing. CULTIVARS AND RELATED SPECIES: *Trillium cuneatum,* wakerobin, is a sessile trillium, meaning the flowers are borne directly on the leaves, with no stalk. The sepals and wine-red petals stick straight up out of the center of the whorl of three mottled leaves. Plants self-sow freely and will bloom in 4 to 5 years. *Trillium erectum,* red trillium, has

blood-red outward-facing flowers held above the wide, pointed leaves on thin stalks. A bright red berry forms in summer, containing a dozen or more seeds.

COMPANION SHRUBS & TREES

Shrubs

Aesculus parviflora—
    Bottlebrush Buckeye
*Amelanchier alnifolia—*Saskatoon
Aronia species—Chokeberries
Callicarpa species—Beautyberries
*Calycanthus floridus—*Carolina Allspice
*Camellia sasanqua—*Autumn Camellia
Cornus rotundifolia—
    Round-leaf Dogwood

MOIST
SHADE

Corylopsis species—Winter Hazels
Diervilla species—Bush Honeysuckles
Dirca palustris—Leatherwood
Enkianthus campanulatus—
     Redvein Enkianthus
Fothergilla species—Witch Alders
Gaultheria shallon—Salal
Hamamelis species—Witchhazels
Hydrangea aspera—Hydrangea
Hydrangea quercifolia—
     Oak-leaf Hydrangea
Leucothoe species—Hobblebushes
Neviusia alabamensis—
     Alabama Snow-wreath
Pieris japonica—Japanese Pieris
Rhododendron prunifolium—
     Plum-leaf Azalea
Rhododendron prinophyllum—
     Rose Azalea
Rhododendron catawbiense—
     Catawba Rhododendron
Styrax japonica—Japanese Snowbell
Styrax americana—American Snowbell
Vaccinium stramineum—Deerberry
Viburnum nudum—Smooth Witherod
Viburnum lentago—Nannyberry
Viburnum acerifolium—Maple-leaf
     Viburnum

Flowering and Small Trees

Acer circinatum—Vine Maple
Acer pensylvanicum—Goosefoot Maple
Acer palmatum—Japanese Maple
Acer spicatum—Mountain Maple
Aesculus pavia—Red Buckeye

Amelanchier species—Serviceberries
Asimina triloba—Pawpaw
Betula alleghaniensis—Yellow Birch
Carpinus caroliniana—Musclewood
Cercis canadensis—Eastern Redbud
Chionanthus virginicus—Fringe Tree
Cladrastis kentuckea—Yellowwood
Clethra acuminata—Cinnamon Clethra
Cornus nuttallii—Pacific Dogwood
Cornus alternifolia—Pagoda Dogwood
Cornus florida—Flowering Dogwood
Halesia carolina (H. tetraptera)—
     Carolina Silverbell
Magnolia sieboldii—Oyama Magnolia
Magnolia tripetala—Umbrella Magnoila
Ostrya virginiana—Hop Hornbeam
Staphylea trifoliata—Bladder Nut
Stewartia species—Stewartias
Styrax obassia—Fragrant Snowbell

Shade Trees

Acer saccharum ssp. grandidentatum—
     Big-tooth Maple
Acer saccharum—Sugar Maple
Aesculus octandra—Yellow Buckeye
Catalpa speciosa—Northern Catalpa
Fagus grandifolia—American Beech
Franklinia alatamaha—Franklinia
Liriodendron tulipifera—Tulip Poplar
Pinus strobus—White Pine
Quercus rubra—Northern Red Oak
Quercus alba— White Oak
Quercus macrocarpa—Bur Oak
Tilia americana—Basswood
Tsuga species—Hemlocks

Perennials for Wet Shade

BY JAMES STEVENSON

Wet shade may *seem* the worst of all possible gardening worlds—gardeners not up to a challenge may dismiss these sites as wastelands. But a wet and shady area can be turned into a lush, thriving, and colorful oasis during summer's doldrums. Perhaps you are fortunate enough to have a low-lying area that stays consistently wet during the growing year, or a site that periodically floods, providing the soil with a changing supply of precious moisture. The real prize is a spring that continually supplies fresh water to your plants. Or you can add a pond to a shady woodland to invite the sun's rays to reflect on the water's shimmering surface; carefully placed perennials and shrubs can accentuate this effect. In any case, there are many wonderful plants for wet shade, from the dramatic to the sublime, including a number of native treasures adapted to naturally occurring seepage slopes, swamps, bottomlands, and flooded forests.

FERNS, GRASSES, & SEDGES

Carex elata 'Bowles' Golden'
BOWLES' GOLDEN SEDGE

Carex elata 'Bowles' Golden'

NATIVE HABITAT AND RANGE: Streamsides and marshes in Eastern Europe

USDA HARDINESS ZONES: 5 to 9, 4 with protection

OUTSTANDING FEATURES: This plant's bright golden foliage is particularly striking in spring, but given plenty of moisture and at least a few hours of sunlight, the gold color will persist through the summer, even in hot areas.

HABIT, USE, AND GOOD COMPANIONS: This 2' by 2', clump-forming accent sedge has many of the softening effects of the more ubiquitous mondo grass, but with a much softer texture, like spun gold. I have seen dramatic sweeps of this underused perennial at the National Arboretum in Washington, D.C. It's very striking at water's edge where the gold/chartreuse color is reflected and amplified. The grassy texture and ever-green habit of many sedges make them perfect companions to broad-leaved plants such as hostas, callas, and Italian arum.

HOW TO GROW: Try growing this grassy perennial in a drainage-free plastic container plunged into a perennial border where the surrounding vegetation provides enough shade to prevent scorching. It will tolerate average soil moisture. Divide in spring, once the clump has grown to a good size.

CULTIVARS AND RELATED SPECIES: There are many lovely, versatile, and hard-working sedges worthy of inclusion in a wet, shady garden. An interesting New Zealander, the hair sedge cultivar *Carex comans* 'Bronze' sports foliage the color of burnished bronze—an "everbrown" that always attracts attention. *C. morrowii,* Japanese sedge (see page 32), is an amazingly attractive clumping sedge with arching leaves that are stiff but graceful. The variegated cultivars 'Gold-band' and 'Variegata' are most appealing.

Cyperus albostriatus
UMBRELLA SEDGE

NATIVE HABITAT AND RANGE: Damp woods and glades in South Africa

USDA HARDINESS ZONES: 7b to 10

OUTSTANDING FEATURES: Umbrella sedge sports sturdy stems topped with a whorl

Cyperus albostriatus 'Variegatus'

of leaves, giving the plant its common name. This very interesting, semi-tender plant is worth overwintering indoors north of its range. It is related to papyrus, the plant Egyptians used to make paper. A mass of stems with their filigree of foliage lends grace and elegance to a quiet pond edge. This is also a great candidate for container culture. Umbrella sedges are widely grown in the Deep South.

HABIT, USE, AND GOOD COMPANIONS: Each stem of a clump will reach 2' in height, and the quickly spreading mass should be allowed plenty of room to grow. If you decide to grow this plant in a container (which makes overwintering indoors much easier), be sure to allow for a large clump. Low, wide galvanized tubs with a few small drainage holes in the bottom or plastic pots work well. This is an ideal companion plant for hostas or other bold-leaved plants like rodgersia or skunk cabbage *(Symplocarpus foetidus)*.

HOW TO GROW: *C. albostriatus* grows in sun or shade. Best when planted or set out in the spring, so that it has an entire growing season to get established. Where hardy, the dwarf umbrella sedge makes an eye-catching groundcover, with an ancient Egyptian look.

CULTIVARS AND RELATED SPECIES: Specialty nurseries carry various umbrella sedges, and you'll have many options to choose from. 'Nanus' is a cute variety that forms a tight groundcover. 'Variegatus' has foliage subtly streaked with cream. *C. alternifolius,* is a taller plant, to 3' to 4' and slightly more tender. There are variegated forms of this species as well.

Dryopteris celsa
LOG FERN

NATIVE HABITAT AND RANGE: Swamps and bottomlands of the Southeast

USDA HARDINESS ZONES: 4 to 9

OUTSTANDING FEATURES: This very architectural fern sends up new foliage early in the year, before many other perennials have woken up. As a result, the 4' fronds tower over the surrounding vegetation, providing soaring verticality. The dark green fronds are lustrous, even shiny, and form beautiful vase-shaped clumps. Each plant remains upright throughout the growing season, and is evergreen through mild winters, but will press its fronds to the ground after the first hard freezes.

HABIT, USE, AND GOOD COMPANIONS: A single specimen makes a statement, but a sweep of this statuesque fern will give a garden visitor pause. Very effective foundation plants around buildings in areas that stay constantly moist, or at the edge of a pond or stream.

HOW TO GROW: Hardy ferns are becoming more widely available, thanks to the efforts of fern enthusiasts, and there are a few nurseries devoted entirely to the propagation, hybridization, and dissemination of this versatile group of plants. Log ferns are worth seeking out for their many garden values. Plant in spring in a humus-rich soil that won't get terribly parched, in dappled to full shade.

CULTIVARS AND RELATED SPECIES: *D. goldiana,* Gold's wood fern, the northern counterpart (found as far north as Minnesota and therefore *much* hardier), is slightly shorter, to 3', with the same glossy thick vase of fronds. *D. ludoviciana,* Southern wood fern, zones 7 to 9, is very similar in appearance but larger, to 5'.

WET SHADE

WET SHADE

Equisetum hyemale
HORSETAIL, SCOURING RUSH

NATIVE HABITAT AND RANGE: Woods and meadows nearly circumpolar in the Northern Hemisphere

USDA HARDINESS ZONES: 2 to 10

OUTSTANDING FEATURES: The horsetails are the surviving members of a group of plants from the era of the dinosaurs. The jointed stems are fresh green, aging to greenish bronze in winter, and very vertical. Stems sport dark rings at each joint, giving a strobe-like effect. Very useful in flower arranging, the sturdy stems, which contain silica (that is, glass), are very rigid, and hold up well.

HABIT, USE, AND GOOD COMPANIONS: This plant has no prominent leaves, but reed-like stems that can grow to a height of 3'. Each stem is topped by a cone-like, spore-bearing structure that looks like the finial on a curtain rod. Caution: You must plant horsetails in a container from which the plant cannot escape. The vigorous juvenile growth speeds through gardens (just like vigorous juvenile humans) and can become quite a nuisance if released (ditto). Simply take the necessary precautions and enjoy this oddity that reflects a bit of our planet's past. Suggested planters: concrete or terra cotta pots with no drainage.

HOW TO GROW: Plant with plenty of room to spread in a soilless, moisture-retentive potting mixture. Often grouped with grasses at the garden centers for lack of a better category, or with aquatics.

CULTIVARS AND RELATED SPECIES: *E. scirpoides*, dwarf scouring rush, attains a height of only 8" to 10" and the cultivar 'Contorta' has curly stems—bizarre and conversation-starting.

Equisetum hyemale

Juncus effusus
RUSH

NATIVE HABITAT AND RANGE: Streamsides and boggy areas worldwide

USDA HARDINESS ZONES: 4 to 9

OUTSTANDING FEATURES: Very striking fountains of stiff but not spiny foliage characterize this grassy plant.

HABIT, USE, AND GOOD COMPANIONS: If you have a naturally wet area in your garden, you probably also have this ubiquitous wetland plant. The strong roots make great stabilizers on a streamside, and the striking foliage—a spherical burst of needle-like leaves that grow to 2'—is topped throughout the summer with interesting bronze flowers. The dark blackish green of the rush contrast well with lighter leaved plants like the chartreusy netted chain fern *(Woodwardia areolata)* and marsh marigold.

HOW TO GROW: Here's another candidate for container gardening; plant in a slow-draining saucer. You can move the potted plant around the garden wherever you need a foil for other plants in season, or leave it in a shady spot on a patio or deck. Placing this along the sides of a pond will secure the banks and provide a safe haven for wildlife. Prefers heavy, wet soils in sun or shade.

CULTIVARS AND RELATED SPECIES: *Juncus* 'Carmen's Gray' has striking gunmetal leaves; *J. effusus* 'Spiralis' is a whirly-curly miniature perfect as a conversation piece.

Maryland and Illinois; also Eurasia

USDA HARDINESS ZONES: 6 to 9

OUTSTANDING FEATURES: Few grasses thrive in shade, but golden millet is one that will cheer up a dismally dark part of the landscape. At 6" to 10" tall, this plant must be planted in drifts, and a mass of it will shine like the sun in a woodland. It produces airy, flowering plumes early in the year, which should be allowed to ripen seed for future generations.

HABIT, USE, AND GOOD COMPANIONS: Use this grass as a skirt around bold-textured plants like ligularia and hosta. It will seed politely hither and yon, and should be encouraged to. Individual plants may be short-lived, so do everything necessary to ensure a long relationship with this charmer.

HOW TO GROW: Purchase plants early in the spring and plant out where they will receive constant moisture and afternoon shade. Plants tolerate more sun in the North.

CULTIVARS AND RELATED SPECIES: *Milium effusum* 'Variegatum', with leaves streaked with creamy white, is reportedly a weak grower.

Milium effusum 'Aureum'
GOLDEN MILLET

NATIVE HABITAT AND RANGE: The species is found along streams and in damp meadows from Quebec and Nova Scotia to

Osmunda regalis
ROYAL FERN (Flowering Fern)

NATIVE HABITAT AND RANGE: Wet woodlands and swamps throughout eastern North America

WET SHADE

WET SHADE

Osmunda regalis

USDA HARDINESS ZONES: 2 to 9

OUTSTANDING FEATURES: Royal fern is a fern to be reckoned with. Bold in appearance, it stands proud, presenting 3' fronds from a single crown, and is vase-shaped in outline. Each frond is composed of narrow, regularly spaced "leaflets," giving it a solid, shrubby look. In late spring some of the fronds produce spore-bearing structures at their tips.

HABIT, USE, AND GOOD COMPANIONS: Use royal fern as a backdrop for other plants. The plumy fronds pair well with heucheras, tiarellas, or some of the early-flowering astilbes. A clump-former, not a runner, royal fern is best used as garden sculpture. A stand of this fern is very dramatic underplanted with bronze sedge, which echoes the color of the spore structure.

HOW TO GROW: If you need a little more moisture for this plant, try lining a 3' x 3' hole with newspaper and filling it with the original soil mixed with some milled sphagnum, topped with a generous layer of mulch or rotted leaves. Otherwise, plant in rich organic soil and plenty of moisture, where this native fern can achieve its statuesque nature. Plants tolerate sun or shade.

CULTIVARS AND RELATED SPECIES: *O. cinnamomea,* the cinnamon fern, is also perfectly at home in a wet, shady garden spot. The fertile fronds of this fern give it its common name, as they are tightly bunched into cinnamon-colored, wand-like structures emerging from the crown of the plant in late spring. The fronds of the cinnamon fern are more highly dissected and therefore more typically fern-like.

Rhynchospora colorata (Dichromena colorata)

WHITE-BRACTED SEDGE

NATIVE HABITAT AND RANGE: Pine savannas and ditches from the North Carolina coast south to the Caribbean

USDA HARDINESS ZONES: 7 to 11

OUTSTANDING FEATURES: Native, white-bracted sedge is unusual in the realm of the grass-like herbs as it produces beautiful and showy white flowers. Long admired in its natural habitat in the Deep South, this sedge makes quite a show of itself when the long, pure white bracts are produced atop strong stems. A mass of these sedges looks like stars fallen to earth; the white is clean and shimmering.

HABIT, USE, AND GOOD COMPANIONS: Another candidate for container use in areas with cold winters; place a pot of this wonderful native in shallow water in the shade for a bright accent in mid-summer when the flowers are at their most spectacular. The stems generally reach a height of 1' to 2' when in flower, the foliage, a lovely apple green, is held at about 8".

HOW TO GROW: Be sure to purchase this protected native grass from a reputable nursery that has propagated, not wild-collected, it. Gardeners in the northern range of this sedge's distribution should buy from a local nursery, as plants from

Rhynchospora colorata

the deeper South may not be suitably hardy. If you decide to grow the plant in a container, be sure to provide a constant source of moisture or you will have crispy fried sedge at the first hint of drought. Thrives in sandy or loamy soil in full sun to partial shade.

CULTIVARS AND RELATED SPECIES: None

Woodwardia areolata
NETTED CHAIN FERN

NATIVE HABITAT AND RANGE: Wet woods and streamsides throughout the eastern U.S.

USDA HARDINESS ZONES: 5 to 9

OUTSTANDING FEATURES: This plant has a texture unique among ferns—not the jade filigree familiar to most as fern-like, but a heavier and more solid texture. On close inspection you'll see the reason for the fern's common name—venation is netted through each leaf.

HABIT, USE, AND GOOD COMPANIONS: Typically this fern grows to a height of 12", but in areas of high fertility or more sunlight, it can grow to 2'. The attractive wide fronds are the sterile fronds. Later in the season, the plant produces fertile fronds with spore-producing structures on the underside. After the spores are released, the fertile fronds turn brown, and create an interesting contrast with the fresh green sterile fronds. You will learn to love this contrast.

HOW TO GROW: Plant chain fern where

WET
SHADE

WET SHADE

you can take advantage of its lovely chartreuse new foliage, which is produced almost year-round as long as

Woodwardia areolata

there is an adequate supply of moisture. The creeping rhizomes will cling to the side of a stream or the edge of a pond in acidic soil. In areas of poor drainage, chain fern will remain in its bounds, circling where the moisture is greatest; fronds will be taller with more sunlight. CULTIVARS AND RELATED SPECIES: *W. virginica* has larger, more finely divided fronds with glossy, black stipes. This fern is at home in very sunny as well as shady sites, as long as these spots remain wet throughout the growing season.

FLOWERING PLANTS

Acorus gramineus
SWEET FLAG
NATIVE HABITAT AND RANGE: Wetlands, bogs, and ponds in Europe, China, and Japan

USDA HARDINESS ZONES: 7 to 10

OUTSTANDING FEATURES: This evergreen, spreading clump makes a great grass-like skirt for other perennials, providing interest during winter, or along the edge of a pond. The variegated and bright golden varieties are very lively and invite the viewer's eye to a shaded area. Sweet flag resembles grassy landscape plants like mondo grass and the sedges, yet it is related to familiar house plants like philodendron and the massive, tropical elephant ears. A spicy aroma comes from calamus oil, long used in the perfume industry; you'll smell it when you brush against the foliage or, if you've planted one of the smaller varieties between stepping stones, when you walk on it.

HABIT, USE, AND GOOD COMPANIONS: The gently arching, 8" to 12" leaves are very graceful and provide a softening effect to corners of buildings or a bend in a shaded path. The plant's fine texture combines well with hostas and other bold-leaved plants. Slightly tender, it may need to be overwintered indoors north of zone 7. Drought or sunlight will burn

Acorus gramineus 'Variegatus'

the foliage, but you can easily remedy this by shearing the plant to the ground for a refreshing flush of new growth.

HOW TO GROW: Look for *Acorus* in the groundcover or grass section of your garden center. Plants are easily divided into smaller sections, so you can often get several specimens out of a single well-grown pot. Best planted in spring, so that it has a long season to get established. Plant right at the edge of a pond, in damp to average soil in the shade, or even in a container plunged into the water.

CULTIVARS AND RELATED SPECIES: 'Ogon' is bright golden chartreuse, 'Pusillus' is diminutive—excellent between stepping stones, and 'Variegatus' has creamy striped foliage that combines beautifully with white calla lilies.

Arisaema triphyllum
JACK-IN-THE-PULPIT

NATIVE HABITAT AND RANGE: Wet floodplain woodlands and along streambanks throughout eastern North America, from southern Canada to Louisiana

USDA HARDINESS ZONES: 4 to 9

OUTSTANDING FEATURES: The charming "jacks" unfurl their three leaflets to provide a parasol for the unique hooded flowers. Over time and with consistent moisture and nutrients, plants may attain a height of 3', but 1½' to 2' is more common. Plants grown in less than ideal conditions will produce only leaves, flowering the following year if conditions improve. After flowering, a club of orange berries develops.

HABIT, USE, AND GOOD COMPANIONS: Every shady garden needs a clump of this native wonder. The curious flowers are wildly different from plant to plant, sometimes with deep purple stripes along the hood, sometimes with small solid purple hoods. The foliage of a well-grown plant will attain a tropical look with the three leaflets spanning 2' across. In late summer, as the fruit matures, it turns a bright orange-red. Often the foliage will begin to go dormant at this stage, leaving the fruit stalk to stand as a beacon in the woodland. Grow a clump of jacks at the base of a tree, where the berries will show off against the trunk. Perfect for the consistently wet shade garden.

HOW TO GROW: Luckily, this plant should be easy to find either from mail-order suppliers or at a well-stocked garden

WET SHADE

WET
SHADE

Arisaema triphyllum

center. Be sure to buy a plant in active growth, and provide a fertile, wet soil when transplanting. Dried tubers are sometimes available, but these might have been collected from the wild and the resulting plants could be weak and slow to flower—not to mention stolen! If you would like to propagate this plant, collect the berries in September and clean the seeds of the fleshy coat (wear rubber gloves and wash the seeds in a bowl of water to facilitate the cleaning process). Sow them in an outdoor seedbed or directly into the garden. First-year seedlings will be small and quickly go dormant, but may be transplanted after dormancy to a suitable spot in the garden. If soil becomes too dry, plants go dormant.

CULTIVARS AND RELATED SPECIES: *A. dracontium,* green dragon, is not quite as adapted to a constantly wet soil, but is well suited to any shade garden. All parts of the plant are more slender than those of Jack-in-the-pulpit, with divided leaflets and a long whip-like extension at the tip of the hood, which often reaches up above the foliage. Very surreal and fascinating.

Caltha palustris
MARSH MARIGOLD

NATIVE HABITAT AND RANGE: Marshes, wet woods, and streamsides throughout the Northern Hemisphere

USDA HARDINESS ZONES: 3 to 10

OUTSTANDING FEATURES: Cheerful yellow buttercup flowers are borne on sturdy stalks early in the spring. The glossy rounded leaves form a nice mound that shows off the flowers.

HABIT, USE, AND GOOD COMPANIONS: Marsh marigold can reach a height of 2' if given plenty of moisture and a rich organic soil, though the typical height tends to be about 1'. This clump-forming perennial looks great in masses or sweeps along the edge of a pond or in a low-lying area. Plant marsh marigold with ferns such as the log fern *(Dryopteris celsa),* whose rich, green leaves will serve as backdrop for the golden flowers. Marsh marigold's green foliage remains attractive throughout the year.

HOW TO GROW: Plants need wet soil in spring, and adapt to drier summer conditions by going dormant. A great candidate for container culture when grown

Caltha palustris

WET
SHADE

in a very slowly draining pot and popped into the landscape wherever the flowers, or later the foliage, can be easily viewed. Pots can also be plunged into ponds and water gardens. Relatively easy to find in the trade, either from a mail-order supplier or garden center.

CULTIVARS AND RELATED SPECIES: 'Multiplex' has double pom-pom-like flowers, and subsequently a longer blooming period, and 'Alba' is bright white, one of those "glow-in-the-dark" plants whose light-colored flowers brighten up the proverbial dark corners of a garden.

Chelone lyonii
TURTLEHEAD
NATIVE HABITAT AND RANGE: Wet woods, seeps, ditches, and along streams in eastern North America

USDA HARDINESS ZONES: 3 to 7

OUTSTANDING FEATURES: The deep green,

Chelone lyonii

toothed foliage is attractive all summer, long before the rosy pink flowers open. Each flower resembles a turtle with a gaping mouth. A dozen or so flowers are carried together in terminal clusters.

HABIT, USE, AND GOOD COMPANIONS: Tallish and stately, the 2' to 4' stems of this native perennial sport their flowers in late summer and autumn. Very effective when planted with *Lobelia siphilitica,* the great blue lobelia, whose tight spikes of blue flowers combine well with the pinkish or white flowers of the turtleheads. Great sweeps are effective in an area of poor drainage, providing midsummer interest when most of the shaded woodland is green.

HOW TO GROW: Plant turtleheads where the flowers can be viewed close up—even if it is during a mad dash inside to get away from the swarms of mosquitoes that always seems to emerge during this plant's flowering season. The plants can be cut back by half in midspring to promote stocky growth and lush foliage. Effective at the edge of a stream or pond where bank stabilization is required. The mat of roots that form as the plant is spreading will hold on to great effect. Flowering is heaviest in light to partial shade.

CULTIVARS AND RELATED SPECIES: *C. obliqua*, purple turtlehead, from the Deep South is adapted to a wide range of conditions. The pinkish mauve flowers are like their sisters'—fancifully shaped like

Erythronium americanum

reptiles. *C. glabra*—narrow leaves and white flowers on thin stems—will travel.

Erythronium americanum
DOG-TOOTH VIOLET (Trout Lily)

NATIVE HABITAT AND RANGE: Wet woodlands, floodplains, and moist coves throughout eastern and central North America

USDA HARDINESS ZONES: 3 to 9

OUTSTANDING FEATURES: The strap-like, mottled foliage would be reason enough to grow this charming spring ephemeral, but in early spring, the beautiful nodding butter-cream flowers, like miniature tiger lilies, take one's breath away. Often found growing in huge masses in wet woodlands; a blanket of dog-tooth violet can convince even the most bitter of cynics that there are things worth living for.

HABIT, USE, AND GOOD COMPANIONS: Brown-patterned foliage emerges in very early spring; the dark coloring collects the sun's warmth and speeds growth. Flowers appear as soon as strong light hits the forest floor—April to May in the Southeast. Try a small patch of dog-tooth violet with another of their ephemeral kin such as spring beauty, whose tiny white flowers look like millions of stars fallen to earth.

HOW TO GROW: Order bulbs from a reputable nursery and plant immediately where you can leave them for years. Plant pointed end down; best planting time is fall.

WET SHADE

CULTIVARS AND RELATED SPECIES: *E. albidum,* white trout lily, is a bit more delicate, with white flowers blushed with blue. Most common in limy soils of the Midwest.

Geranium maculatum
WILD GERANIUM

NATIVE HABITAT AND RANGE: Wet meadows, prairies, and floodplain woods throughout eastern and central North America

USDA HARDINESS ZONES: 3 to 9

OUTSTANDING FEATURES: Perennial geraniums have at last become popular in this country. The wonderful foliage has been likened to paper cut-out snowflakes, often very deeply lobed though overall round in outline. Handsome mounds of foliage are produced after a long season of bloom. The 1" saucer-shaped flowers are held in clusters high above the foliage and are a lovely pinkish purple.

HABIT, USE, AND GOOD COMPANIONS: Early

flowering, neat and tidy, this cottage garden favorite should be planted where its flowers won't be obscured by surrounding vegetation.

HOW TO GROW: Grows equally well in full sun or full shade, in rich soil. Self-sown seedlings are often plentiful. You will have plenty to trade.

CULTIVARS AND RELATED SPECIES: 'Hazel Gallagher' has frosty white flowers; 'Chatto', a new cultivar from England, has splendid, pale pink flowers.

Hosta plantaginea
FRAGRANT PLANTAIN LILY

NATIVE HABITAT AND RANGE: Low woods and seeps in China

USDA HARDINESS ZONES: 3 to 9

OUTSTANDING FEATURES: Hostas are popular landscape and garden plants with lush, bold foliage that stays attractive all summer long. An added feature of this clump-forming perennial is its propensity for wet areas. Fragrant white flowers are produced on tall scapes in midsummer.

HABIT, USE, AND GOOD COMPANIONS: Hostas are denizens of meadows and streamsides, and the adaptable *Hosta plantaginea* will tolerate extreme moisture. The foliage is bold and applegreen, and forms a 2' by 3' clump. Masses are stunning. The flowers are produced atop 4' stems and resemble tiny lilies, to which hostas are related.

Geranium maculatum

Hosta plantaginea

The delicate textures of ferns and sedges contrast well with large-leaved hostas and will provide some winter interest if well selected.

HOW TO GROW: Be sure to place this hosta where the fragrance of the summer flowers can be enjoyed. Suitable for the edge of a shaded path in average to wet conditions, or along a stream or pondside. Equally at home in moist to wet soil, this hosta grows like a weed once established. The huge clumps will need dividing to keep them under control, unless they are planted on their own, away from garden companions.

CULTIVARS AND RELATED SPECIES: 'Aphrodite' has stunning, double white flowers. 'Grandiflora' has congested clumps of long tubular flowers at the top of squat stalks. 'Honeybells' has purple-tinted flowers in August. 'Royal Standard' has pure white flowers and is a little less vigorous.

Ligularia stenocephala
LIGULARIA, GOLDEN-RAY

NATIVE HABITAT AND RANGE: Along mountain streams and in wet areas in China and Japan

USDA HARDINESS ZONES: 4 to 8

OUTSTANDING FEATURES: Big, bold foliage and interesting golden flowers have made this plant popular in northern and European gardens for years. The pancake-sized leaves have sharply toothed edges, and are a dramatic deep green. In late summer, spires of golden flowers thrust up out of the shade like candles, lighting the way through the forest.

HABIT, USE, AND GOOD COMPANIONS: Each leaf arises from a central crown on a sturdy stalk, and clumps can become 3' across over time. The shiny mound of foliage becomes a great support for the assertive flower display.

HOW TO GROW: Site this perennial where you can enjoy its foliar attributes as well as the opulent display of flowers late in the season. Plenty of moisture to a constantly wet soil will ensure the largest leaves and best flowering.

CULTIVARS AND RELATED SPECIES: 'The Rocket' is probably easier to find than the species. 'Zepter' is a hybrid with thick, sparsely toothed leaves and huge spikes to 6'; larger and more robust. *L. dentata* 'Othello' and 'Desdemona' are purple-leaved selections that bear flowers in flat-topped clusters rather than

WET SHADE

WET
SHADE

Ligularia dentata 'Othello'

wands. *Farfugium japonicum (L. tussilaginea)* will actually thrive in the South; its cultivar 'Aureomaculatum' has irregular golden spots in the leaves, while 'Crispatum' has leaves that are crinkle-cut around the edges.

Lilium canadense
MEADOW LILY

NATIVE HABITAT AND RANGE: Wet woods and meadows in New England south to the Appalachian Mountains

USDA HARDINESS ZONES: 4 to 8

OUTSTANDING FEATURES: Nodding orange lilies are a sight to behold in summer. A blaze of orange when in flower, with foliage arranged in tiers along the tall stems. This species—and other native treasures—deserves wider use, so encourage your nursery to grow them.

HABIT, USE, AND GOOD COMPANIONS: Well-grown plants can soar to 9', so plan accordingly. If you are fortunate enough to have several of these bulbs, a sweep of them would be breathtaking; otherwise combine with sturdy shrubs that can support the slender stems.

HOW TO GROW: Be sure to plant this coveted bulb where it will receive constant moisture, especially in the summer, as well as support either from neighboring shrubs or stakes. Sometimes the stems are so laden with flowers they have the tendency to just give up and come crashing to earth.

Lilium canadense

WET SHADE

WET
SHADE

CULTIVARS AND RELATED SPECIES: *L. super-bum,* turk's cap lily, another native orange lily; culture and habit are the same, but it might enjoy a slightly sunnier spot. Hardy to zone 4.

Lobelia cardinalis
CARDINAL FLOWER

NATIVE HABITAT AND RANGE: Along streams and in wet meadows in eastern and central North America

USDA HARDINESS ZONES: 2 to 9

OUTSTANDING FEATURES: Are you having trouble coaxing hummingbirds and butterflies into your shaded garden? Try a patch of this native wildflower or one of its many cousins, and watch the wildlife move in. Stately spires of bright crimson flowers are produced for weeks in summer. Each flower looks like a little hummingbird in flight (imagination required).

HABIT, USE, AND GOOD COMPANIONS: In late spring, the winter rosette begins its rise to glory, and the thick stem slowly elongates, finally topping itself in cardinal blooms. The true red color is very striking and combines well with chartreuse-leaved plants. Grow cardinal flowers along the edge of a stream, allowing them to poke up past gold-leaved hostas. After flowering, the seed pods swell with millions of tiny bronze seeds. Let some come up around the parent plant to create a dramatic colony.

Lobelia cardinalis

HOW TO GROW: Cardinal flower grows from a wide basal rosette of foliage that must remain free of mulch or debris through the winter. Leave this rosette exposed to enjoy the russet color of the foliage. Site cardinal flower where you can view the crimson flowers backlit. Demands rich soil in sun or shade.

CULTIVARS AND RELATED SPECIES: *L. siphilitica,* the great blue lobelia, is slightly shorter in stature, and holds its many flowers in tight bunches on stocky 18" stems. Great blue-violet flower color plays off the golds of mid-summer when it is in flower.

Primula japonica
JAPANESE PRIMROSE

NATIVE HABITAT AND RANGE: Along mountain streams throughout Japan

Primula japonica

USDA HARDINESS ZONES: 5 to 9

OUTSTANDING FEATURES: Gorgeous, tall, and stately, this candelabra-type primrose is so called because the flowers are held on ascendant sturdy stems. Flower colors range from white to pale pink to rose and purple. The white selections seem pale yellow owing to the dark yellow eye at the center of each flower.

HABIT, USE, AND GOOD COMPANIONS: Tightly packed clusters of flowers are arranged in several tiers along the tall stems. The Japanese primrose is in bloom for what seems like an eternity in spring. Very nice in consort with Louisiana iris, which can be found in the same pastel shades.

HOW TO GROW: Plant this species primrose at water's edge, where the flowers will be reflected on the surface. Or simply spot a few through a woodland, letting them send up their spheres of flowers, and seeding where the ground is the moistest. Very easy in most soils. Plants self sow freely.

CULTIVARS AND RELATED SPECIES: There are a few pure color strains, but the natural range of colors really is self-complementary.

Rodgersia pinnata
RODGERSIA

NATIVE HABITAT AND RANGE: Wet woodlands and streamsides and pond edges in western China

USDA HARDINESS ZONES: 4 to 7

OUTSTANDING FEATURES: Dramatic, lush, heavily textured foliage resembling the hand-shaped leaves of the horse chestnut (no relation) with sumptuous fall colors make this long-lived perennial the envy of southern gardeners. Each leaf can reach a width of 12", and the prominent venation adds interest throughout the season. Big plumes of pink flowers are produced in summer, followed by russet fruits.

HABIT, USE, AND GOOD COMPANIONS: Structural plants for water's edge or bog garden, the sturdy clumps can reach 4' in width and height. They are most effective as a focal point or accent, with plenty of room to develop to full size. Use ferns, grasses, and sedges to contrast with the bold leaves. Combine with

WET SHADE

WET SHADE

Rodgersia pinnata 'Superba'

spiky flowers such as cardinal flower.

HOW TO GROW: Plant rodgersia where the roots will never dry out. Plants do best in partial shade or dappled light. Unsightly leaf scorching may occur during periods of drought or if leaves are exposed to direct hot sun. Protect the huge, exposed crowns from damaging bitter, cold wind in northern zones.

CULTIVARS AND RELATED SPECIES: 'Superba' is exuberant in all respects; it has deep rose pink flowers. *R. podophylla* has bronze-tinted leaves with coarse teeth at the end of each foot-long leaflet and white flowers. *R. sambucifolia* has large, deep green, pinnate leaves resembling those of the elderberry.

Symplocarpus foetidus
SKUNK CABBAGE

NATIVE HABITAT AND RANGE: Swamps, seepages, and wet woodlands throughout the Northeast and Midwest, south into the mountains

USDA HARDINESS ZONES: 4 to 7

OUTSTANDING FEATURES: One of the first of the wildflowers to bloom; the interesting hooded flowers often poke out of the snow, which they actually melt away as the flowers produce heat. The dark purple, hooded flowers also soak up the sun's rays, keeping their interiors warm and attractive to the earliest of pollinators. Big rosettes of foliage follow flowering and persist throughout the growing season.

HABIT, USE, AND GOOD COMPANIONS: The winter flowers of skunk cabbage herald the coming of spring, and true plant enthusiasts love them as only mothers can. Certainly not the kind of flower one might pick for a hostess's bouquet—the real drama comes after flowering, when the 2', heart-shaped foliage unfurls, forming a handsome rosette. This bold and beautiful texture combines well with ferns and other delicate plants like its cousin, sweet flag.

HOW TO GROW: Skunk cabbage may be hard to find in garden centers, but check native plant nurseries, and keep alert to plant rescue efforts. These wonderful curiosities will thrive at the edge of a pond or stream in dappled to full shade.

CULTIVARS AND RELATED SPECIES: *Lysichiton americanum,* yellow skunk cabbage, is the western counterpart to *Symplocarpus*, growing from San Francisco to Alaska along the coast. The flowers of this plant are larger than those of skunk cabbage, and warm yellow, opening in April along with the emerging foliage. Difficult to grow in the Southeast; best left to areas with cooler summers.

Veratrum viride
WILD HELLEBORE

NATIVE HABITAT AND RANGE: Moist to wet woodlands and bogs in northeastern North America

USDA HARDINESS ZONES: 3 to 7

OUTSTANDING FEATURES: Bold, attractive,

Symplocarpus foetidus

WET SHADE

Veratrum viride

pleated foliage makes a strong and unique statement in the wet shade garden. Wild hellebore provides interesting foliage as well as a plume of greenish flowers in midsummer. Very seldom encountered in gardens in this country. Be careful if young children frequent your garden—all parts of this plant are toxic.

HABIT, USE, AND GOOD COMPANIONS: The striking foliage of the wild hellebore (no relation to true hellebore, by the way) rises to 3', alternating along either side of the stem. In summer, delightful fluffy plumes of greenish flowers resembling those of astilbe appear above the stems. After flowering the foliage tends to become a little tattered; you may wish to site this plant where more delicate and fresher-looking plants can conceal this natural occurrence. A ruff of sedges would do the job nicely along a natural or artificial stream or pond. Constant

moisture will ensure strong stocky plants with healthier foliage.

HOW TO GROW: This plant may be a little hard to track down; check native plant nurseries and seed exchanges. Slow to flower from seed, but you may be the proud parent of a healthy patch of wild hellebore with a few years' patience. Plant in peaty soil where a constant supply of moisture can be counted on, and leave undisturbed.

CULTIVARS AND RELATED SPECIES: Several other species have been described and used in European gardens for years. Two white-flowered species, *V. album* from Europe and the native *V. californicum*, with huge white flower clusters, might be fun to try in the cooler parts of the country. Dramatic *V. nigrum* has oxblood flowers.

COMPANION SHRUBS & TREES

Shrubs

Andromeda polifolia—Bog Rosemary
Aralia spinosa—Hercules Club
Aronia arbutifolia—Chokeberry
Cephalanthus occidentalis—Buttonbush
Chamaedaphne calyculata—Leatherleaf
Clethra alnifolia—Summersweet,
     Sweet Pepperbush
Cornus stolonifera (C. sericea)—
     Red-twig Dogwood

Cyrilla racemiflora—Titi
Decodon verticillatus—Water Willow
Dirca palustris—Leatherwood
Ilex amelanchier—Sarvis Holly
Illicium floridanum—
   Florida Anise Bush
Itea virginica—Virginia Sweetspire
Ledum groenlandicum—Labrador Tea
Leucothoe racemosa—Sweetbells
Lindera benzoin—Spicebush
Myrica cerifera—Wax Myrtle
Osmanthus americanus—Devilwood
Rhododendron serrulatum—
   Hammocksweet
Rhododendron viscosum—Swamp Azalea
Rosa carolina—Carolina Rose
Salix elaeagnos—Rosemary Willow
Salix melanostachys—Black Pussywillow
Salix purpurea—Purple Osier Willow
Sambucus canadensis—Elderberry
Spiraea alba—White Spiraea
Spiraea tomentosa—Hardhack
Vaccinium corymbosum—
   Highbush Blueberry
Vaccinium macrocarpon—Cranberry
Viburnum dentatum—Arrowwood
Viburnum opulus—Cranberry Bush
Zenobia pulverulenta—Dusty Zenobia

Flowering and Small Trees

Alnus serrulata—Tag Alder
Amelanchier canadensis—Shadblow,
   Serviceberry
Asimina triloba—Pawpaw

Betula nigra—River Birch
Chionanthus virginicus—Fringe Tree
Cornus alternifolia—Pagoda Dogwood
Magnolia grandiflora—
   Bull Bay Magnolia
Magnolia virginiana—
   Sweet Bay Magnolia
Persea borbonia—Red Bay
Staphylea trifolia—Bladdernut
Stewartia ovata—Stewartia

Shade Trees

Acer negundo—Box Elder
Acer saccharinum—Silver Maple
Carya aquatica—Water Hickory
Fraxinus caroliniana—Ash
Gleditsia aquatica—Water Locust
Gymnocladus dioicus—
   Kentucky Coffee Tree
Larix laricina—Eastern Larch
Nyssa sylvatica—Black Gum, Tupelo
Platanus occidentalis—Sycamore
Populus heterophylla—Cottonwood
Quercus lyrata—Overcup Oak
Quercus palustris—Pin Oak
Quercus phellos—Willow Oak
Salix alba—White Willow
Salix babylonica—Weeping Willow
Taxodium ascendens—Pond Cypress
Taxodium distichum—Bald Cypress

HARDINESS ZONE MAP

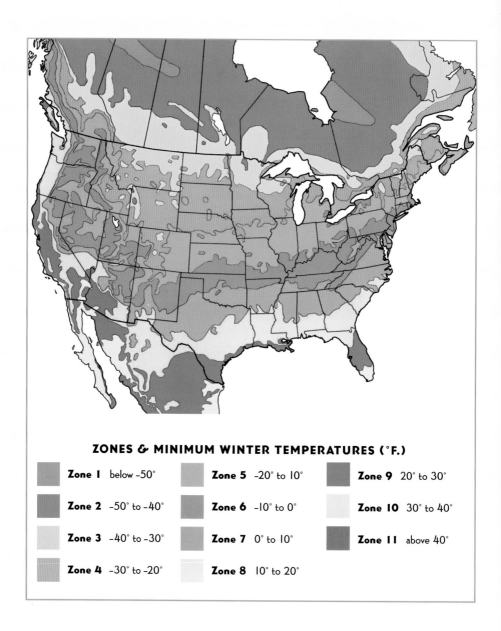

ZONES & MINIMUM WINTER TEMPERATURES (°F.)

Zone 1 below -50°

Zone 2 -50° to -40°

Zone 3 -40° to -30°

Zone 4 -30° to -20°

Zone 5 -20° to 10°

Zone 6 -10° to 0°

Zone 7 0° to 10°

Zone 8 10° to 20°

Zone 9 20° to 30°

Zone 10 30° to 40°

Zone 11 above 40°

Armitage, Allan. *Herbaceous Perennial Plants.* Stipes Publishing, Champagne, IL 1997.

Bir, Richard E. *Growing and Propagating Showy Native Woody Plants.* University of North Carolina Press, Chapel Hill, 1992.

Burrell, C. Colston. *A Gardener's Encyclopedia of Wildflowers.* Rodale Press, Emmaus, PA, 1997.

Burrell, C. Colston, ed. *Ferns: Wild Things Make a Comeback in the Garden.* Brooklyn Botanic Garden, NY, 1994.

Burrell, C. Colston, ed. *Woodland Gardens: Shade Gets Chic.* Brooklyn Botanic Garden, NY, 1995.

Chatto, Beth. *The Green Tapestry.* Collier Books, NY, 1988. Also *The Damp Garden* and *The Dry Garden.*

Druse, Ken. *The Natural Shade Garden.* Clarkson Potter, NY, 1992.

Ferreniea, Viki. *Wildflowers in Your Garden.* Random House, NY, 1993.

Fish, Margery. *Gardening in the Shade.* Faber and Faber, London, 1964.

Glattstein, Judy. *Enhance Your Garden with Japanese Plants.* Kodansha International, NY, 1996.

Hinkley, Daniel. *The Explorer's Garden.* Timber Press, Portland, 1999.

Lloyd, Christopher. *Foliage Plants.* Random House, NY, 1973.

Lovejoy, Ann. *The American Mixed Border.* Macmillan, NY, 1993.

Lovejoy, Ann. *Naturalistic Gardening.* Sasquatch Books, Seattle, 1998.

Morse, Harriet K. *Gardening in the Shade.* Timber Press, Beaverton, OR, 1982.

Mickel, John. *Ferns for American Gardens.* Macmillan, NY, 1994.

Miles, Bebe. *Wildflower Perennials for Your Garden.* Hawthorne Books, NY, 1976.

Phillips, Ellen and C. Colston Burrell. *Rodale's Illustrated Encyclopedia of Perennials.* Rodale Press, Emmaus, PA, 1993.

Phillips, Harry R. *Growing and Propagating Wild Flowers.* The University of North Carolina Press, Chapel Hill, 1985.

Phillips, Roger and Martin Rix. *Perennials.* Random House, NY, 1991.

Wasowski, Sally. *Gardening with Native Plants of the South.* Taylor Publishing Co., Dallas, 1994.

AMBERGATE GARDENS
8730 County Rd 43
Chaska, MN 55318
952-443-2248
www.ambergategardens.com

ARROWHEAD ALPINES
1310 N. Gregory Rd
Fowlerville, MI 48836
517-223-3581
www.arrowheadalpines.com

CANYON CREEK NURSERY
3527 Dry Creek Road
Oroville, CA 95965
530-533-2166
www.canyoncreeknursery.com

COLLECTOR'S NURSERY
16804 NE 102nd Street
Battleground, WA 98604
360-574-3832
www.collectorsnursery.com

DIGGING DOG NURSERY
PO Box 471
Albion, CA 95410
707-937-1130
www.diggingdog.com

FANCY FRONDS
PO Box 1090
Gold Bar, WA 98251
360-793-1472
www.fancyfronds.com

FOLIAGE GARDENS
2003 128th Ave SE
Bellevue, WA 98005
425-747-2998
www.foliagegardens.com

FOREST FARM
990 Tetherow Rd
Williams, OR 97544
541-846-7269
fax 541-846-6963
www.forestfarm.com

HERONSWOOD NURSERY
7530 NE 288th Street
Kingston, WA 98346
360-297-4172
www.heronswood.com

JOY CREEK NURSERY
20300 NW Watson Road
Scappoose, OR 97056
503-543-7474
www.joycreek.com

NATIVE GARDENS
5737 Fisher Lane
Greenback, TN 37742
865-856-0220
www.native-gardens.com

PLANT DELIGHTS NURSERY
9241 Sauls Rd
Raleigh, NC 27603
919-772-4794
www.plantdelights.com

PRIMROSE PATH
921 Scottdale-Dawson Rd
Scottdale, PA 15683
724-887-6756
www.theprimrosepath.com

ROSLYN NURSERY
211 Burrs Lane
Dix Hills, NY 11746
631-643-9347
www.roslynnursery.com

SISKIYOU RARE PLANT NURSERY
2825 Cummings Rd
Medford, OR 97501
541-772-6846
www.srpn.net

SUNLIGHT GARDENS
174 Golden Lane
Andersonville, TN 37705
800-272-7396
www.sunlightgardens.com

WE-DU NURSERIES
2055 Polly Spout Rd
Marion, NC 28752
828-738-8300
www.we-du.com

WOODLANDER'S INC.
1128 Colleton Avenue
Aiken, SC 29801
803-648-7522

C. Colston Burrell is a garden designer, writer, and photographer. A lifelong gardener and advocate for native plants, he has written and taught about plant identification, garden use, and propagation for over 20 years. He is author of *A Gardener's Encyclopedia of Wildflowers* and is president of Native Landscape Design and Restoration, Ltd. of Minneapolis, which specializes in landscape restoration and the creation of environmentally appropriate gardens.

Edith Eddleman is a garden designer, writer, and lecturer from Durham, North Carolina. Since 1982, she has been the volunteer designer and co-curator of the perennial border at the J.C. Raulston Arboretum at North Carolina State University.

Lucy Hardiman is a garden designer, writer, teacher, and speaker. She has written articles for *Fine Gardening, Garden Showcase, The Oregonian,* and *Pacific Northwest Gardener,* and her own garden has appeared in *Better Homes and Garden, Fine Gardening, The Oregonian,* and *Victorian Home.* She has also taught and spoken at Portland State University, and the Portland, Seattle and San Francisco Flower Shows, and is president of the Hardy Plant Society of Oregon.

Charles and Martha Oliver are the owners of The Primrose Path, a mail-order company in southwestern Pennsylvania that specializes in primulas, heucheras, heucherellas, tiarellas, and other native and exotic woodland plants. Charles runs the mail-order portion of the nursery and tissue-culture laboratory and maintains a breeding and selection program. Martha has a garden design business: She installs woodland gardens and large prairie meadows.

Judy Springer started gardening at age seven, and currently gardens on a 2.5-acre lot in a heavily wooded residential area in northern Virginia, primarily in a shaded woodland setting. Her favorite plants are those with low light requirements, especially hostas. She has a large collection of natives, as well as many Japanese counterparts of indigenous species.

James Stevenson has worked as an intern at the North Carolina Botanical Garden, and as a gardener, nursery manager, and garden center manager at Fearrington Gardens in Pittsboro, North Carolina. He is currently garden curator at Juniper Level Botanic Garden, part of Plant Delights Nursery, Inc., in Raleigh, North Carolina.

ILLUSTRATION CREDITS

Alan & Linda Detrick: pages 16, 25 top, 26, 40, 42, 49, 58, 68, 69, 77, and 80

C. Colston Burrell: pages 1, 24, 43, 61, 63, 73, 74, 92 and 94

Jerry Pavia: 25 bottom, 32, 45, 46, 47, 51, 52, 56, 59, 66, 79, 84, 85, 87, 93, and 98

Pamela Harper: pages 39, 41, 81,

Ken Druse: cover and pages 9, 10, 13, 14, 20, 23, 27, 29, 33, 37, 55, 65, 70, 71, 75, 89, 90, 95, 96, and 100

Derek Fell: pages 4, 35, and 83

Susan Glascock: pages 62, 88, 91, 95 and 99

INDEX

BROOKLYN BOTANIC GARDEN

MICHAEL FUSCO

World renowned for pioneering gardening information, Brooklyn Botanic Garden's 21st-Century Gardening Series of award-winning guides provides spectacularly photographed, compact, practical advice for gardeners in every region of North America.

To order other fine titles published by BBG, call 718-623-7286, or shop in our online store at www.bbg.org/gardenemporium. For more information on Brooklyn Botanic Garden, including an online tour, visit www.bbg.org or call 718-623-7200.

MORE BOOKS ON SHADE GARDENING

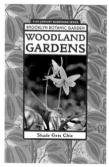